The Power of Letting Go

Discover Inner Peace Opens You To Life's Beauty

While every precaution has been taken in the preparation of this book, the publisher assumes no responsibility for errors or omissions, or for damages resulting from the use of the information contained herein.

THE POWER OF LETTING GO A PRACTICAL GUIDE TO EMOTIONAL HEALING AND MINDFUL LIVING

First edition. February 5, 2024.

ISBN: 979-8224239900

Written by Hadi hans.

Table of Contents

Dedication

Dedicated with love and gratitude to:

My family for their unwavering support, encouragement, and belief in me. You kept me going through this journey.

My beloved wife, Nisreen – your profound love, wisdom, and patience nourishes my soul daily. Thank you for walking this path as my faithful partner.

My precious daughters, Loryan and Loseen – you are my brightest lights. I'm so honored to be your father. Never stop reaching for your dreams!

My friends who listened, advised, laughed, and inspired me as I put these words onto paper over months of effort. This book wouldn't have blossomed without you!

To all those challenging yet nurturing life circumstances and relationships that gave deeper meaning to the messages within this book through lessons of letting go – I embrace you.

Finally, to all past and future readers likewise seeking the keys of liberation and inner peace – may you discover powerful freedom through applying what you learn in these pages.

With Love and Appreciation,

"Introduction for the book "The power of Letting Go

Does your past continue to haunt you? Do you struggle with forgiving others—or even yourself? Do regrets, worries and anger weigh you down? If so, you're not alone. Most people have experienced deep wounds, resentment and fear that won't seem to loosen their grip.

Holding onto our hurts and mistakes is a heavy burden that robs us of joy, ruins relationships, and causes chronic stress. Yet letting go seems difficult, if not Impossible for most of us. We tell ourselves that forgetting the past means we've somehow accepted or excused injustice. Or we worry that releasing anxieties will leave us unprepared and vulnerable. However, emerging research shows the opposite Is true. There is a real art to letting go that brings profound healing, empowerment and inner peace.

In The Art of Letting Go, you'll learn research-backed and scientifically proven techniques to embrace forgiveness, live fully in the present, and build emotional resilience. With clear, practical guidance, letting go will become easy—even natural—by following the five-step journey in this book:

Understand Why You Must Let Go

Too often we underestimate the toll of clinging to emotional wounds and the past. Part One covers eye-opening studies on how dwelling on hurts, mistakes and anger literally shortens lives while contributing to ulcers, hypertension and lowered immunity. You'll discover astounding facts on why those who forgive enjoy better quality relationships, less anxiety and depression, improved sleep health, and live as much as 10 years !longer

Cultivate Acceptance and Forgiveness

Forgiving others is one of the greatest struggles in the human experience. The same goes for self-forgiveness too. Building acceptance and offering forgiveness will be your focus In Part Two. You'll find scripts and step-by-step advice on having courageous conversations and making amends. Plus, an entire chapter covers potent self-forgiveness mantras and techniques endorsed by top therapists when shame and regret are holding .you back

Live in the Now

We human beings sure love living in the past and worrying about the future! Part Three offers you the keys to residing fully in the present moment—which is the only real way to properly live. The book introduces handy mindfulness tricks you can do anytime, anywhere to halt destructive thoughts about what might have been or what could go wrong next. You'll learn how to tune into your senses, appreciate every experience, and see past and future thinking for what they really are: distractions .robbing you of the here and now

Let Go of Future Fears

You may have heard that worry helps us prepare and plan ahead. However, science shows that excessive worrying actually backfires! In Part Four, discover how to discern helpful vs

2

unhelpful fears about tomorrow. You'll be equipped with techniques derived from exposure therapy and cognitive behavioral approaches to nip anxious thoughts in the bud and build your tolerance to uncertainty.

Maintain Peace After Letting Go

Alas, letting go Is not a one-and-done process. Life Inevitably brings new hurts and worries over time. In Part Five, you'll focus on setting healthy boundaries with people, finding self-validation so that you don't regress back to seeking external approval, and responding thoughtfully (not reacting) when life gets rocky. The book's final chapter is filled with joyful guided meditations, self-care rituals, and celebrating how magnificent life feels with Inner peace and emotional freedom!

By the journey's end, you'll feel a weight lifted after releasing years of unnecessary burdens. Letting go liberates you to live each moment to the fullest with optimism, wisdom and wonder like you did as a child. Turn the page to begin

Chapter 1 – The High Cost of Holding On

They say time heals all wounds. But simply waiting for the years to pass doesn't necessarily dissolve anger, erase regrets, or make us forgive those who caused harm. Time only pushes painful memories from immediate awareness into our subconscious. There they lurk, fully intact and capable of sabotaging our happiness, health and relationships.

Decades of resentment toward an absent parent can flare up when you have a child yourself. You promised yourself you wouldn't be bitter about a bad childhood or failed marriage anymore. Yet you catch yourself making snide remarks that convey buried hurt. Anger and bitterness from being mistreated at work in the past boil up when facing new challenges. You dread family events because of the fake smile you have to wear around relatives who once betrayed your trust.

Make no mistake, sweeping pains under the mental rug never works. A University of Virginia study found that people who don't practice self-forgiveness tend to ruminate more on their regrets a decade later compared to those who make peace. Unresolved anger and disappointment haunts us for years. Letting go is the only way forward.

Health Dangers of Holding On

More concerning is how clinging to negative emotions, past failures and old wounds can seriously damage your physical and mental health. Mayo Clinic research reveals that chronic anger triples your risk of heart attack. And bitter people are twice as likely to have strokes or die earlier.

- 3x higher risk of heart disease

- 2x more susceptible to infectious illness

- 75% higher anxiety rates

- 60% increased depression odds

Why does stewing over the words during a fight 10 years ago still plague millions today? Yale psychologists explain that dredging up painful memories triggers our body's primal responses as if we're back in that unpleasant moment. Our muscles tense, breathing intensifies, blood pressure skyrockets, immunity drops and vital systems switch their focus to immediate survival. That's why prolonged stress has been called the #1 threat to health.

Now magnify those daily stress spikes times months or years. The compound damage exceeds what most can endure. Stanford studies found that those who forgive enjoy markedly better heart health across their lifespan. Plus they benefit from 30% lower rates of illness. This makes letting go quite literally life saving.

The Price We Pay

Of course strained relationships, lost joy and debilitating worry continue being perhaps the steepest prices of all. A Columbia University study found that holding onto grievances or hurts often leads to "relationship limbo". We become stuck because our body never gets the signal to fully bond again after conflicts or mistakes occur. That explains why rehashing the past destroys intimacy. Partners who cite past betrayals as proof "you'll never change" strangle hopes of reconciliation and building trust. Resentment is toxic.

Equally serious is how endlessly replaying your mistakes compartmentalizes your self-worth. People describe the regret and shame loop from a failed marriage or losing their career as "hitting rock bottom". You forget dozens of other roles and joys in your life because of fixating on one regret. Thus we sentence ourselves to misery until making peace with imperfections.

The bottom-line is that we sacrifice far too much in vain attempts to deny or cling to life's pains and disappointments. The path forward rests in letting go…

Chapter 2 – Why We Struggle to Let Things Go

If letting go brings such astounding benefits then why do so few seem to master it? As it turns out this inner peace skill gets trained out of us early. Toddlers intrinsically forgive and move past emotional injuries quickly. But well-meaning adults teach little ones to "use their words" and handle mistreatment through confrontation. Studies show the average preschooler forgives someone in under 5 minutes. Whereas adults average 2-3 days after conflicts large or small.

We incorrectly assume that dwelling forces accountability which prevents future harm. However it often backfires. Nursing resentments pressures the offender to defend themselves. So real reconciliation stalls while pain festers. Anger and bitterness then cascade into too many areas of life until letting go finally occurs years later. Interestingly, a University of Miami study found couples who argue to resolve conflicts experience lower relationship satisfaction overall compared to those who make amends quicker.

Beyond childhood coaching, our minds cling to painful thoughts due to psychological biases. Rumination feels productive so we repeat it. The exaggerate, personalize and overgeneralize habits twist perception leading us to fixate on things unfairly. Fears whisper that forgiving too easily invites further mistreatment. Worst of all victim mentalities blind us to healing. We unconsciously enjoy pity and playing small to avoid facing future hurts.

Additionally, lacking self awareness keeps us stuck. We don't recognize root wounds driving anger like abandonment issues, betrayal trauma, codependency or narcissistic injury. We live life from these juvenile emotional states yet wonder why moving on from adulthood conflicts remains impossible. Becoming conscious of shields, blind spots and conditioning is essential.

We may tell ourselves the platitude "forgive and forget" without appreciating the work involved. You must feel in order to heal. Letting go doesn't mean skipping necessary steps like healthy boundaries or speaking truth. It does however require surrendering anger and resistance so we stop hurting too. Understanding these psychological traps and taking responsibility for our reaction is the precursor to release. The coming chapters will unpack all of this and more. For now appreciate that letting go goes against modern conditioning. But we all can learn; and the joyful lives of those who do confirms why it's so worth it...

Chapter 3 – The Peace That Comes from Letting Go

We get so distracted by perceived justice, protecting feelings or our ego's need to be right that we scarcely notice how agony from past hurts decreases daily when we let them go. Those who've walked the path describe many overt rewards on the other side that makes surrendering anger worthwhile.

The most obvious benefit is reclaiming your life's passion after resentment held your dreams hostage. Kiley carried her grief for decades after her ex-husband abandoned her while raising their infant son alone. Though remarried now, his betrayal left her fearful to connect deeply again. She describes her evolution beautifully: "Getting past the anger opened my heart back up. I learned the risks of intimacy are worth it to not lock out love."

Letting go also builds self confidence and courage. No longer defining yourself as someone's victim or blown opportunities as character flaws reduces self judgement. Playing small to avoid rejection loses its hold. Trying new things seems fun rather than intimidating. You recognize healthy risks vs real threats clearly. Emotionally strong people forgive easier because they don't personalize others' actions on themselves. Their stability comes from within rather than appearances, achievements or treatment by others.

Health enthusiasts applaud letting go's physical perks like lower cortisol, stabilized glucose levels and improved cardiovascular health markers. However the mental health gains prove equally profound. Released obsession about why someone hurt you or why you made certain mistakes lowers anxiety and catastrophic thinking. Making peace with imperfections prevents spinning worries that you are flawed, unlovable or destined to fail.

Letting go also bears a hidden blessing: freedom from other's actions. When we resent others' behavior, in truth we resent their freedom to behave as they choose. Forgiveness surrenders the illusion that we can control people. We regain power not by demanding change but realizing love stays steady regardless what others say or do. This principle works miracles to stabilize relationships.

Indeed, the personal tranquility found from letting go ripples outwards to benefit every relationship. Tolerating personality quirks instead of fault finding brings you closer to friends and family. Colleagues pick up on the grace and gravitate towards it. Romantic partners notice how you correct misunderstandings quickly before they escalate like in the past. We teach people how to treat us. Demonstrating quick forgiveness sets the tone for respect.

Do pleasant memories surface about who you were before adversity hit? Many describe their former self as enthusiastic, trusting and quick to smile. Holding onto pain changes you. Letting it go allows your essence to shine again. People often emerge happier on the other side of forgiveness still bearing the wisdom gained by difficulties without being burdened by bitterness. We all know ostensibly "happy" people who seem a bit lifeless behind the eyes and plastered on grins. True joy radiates from peace within.

This peace primes you to receive life's other graces. Chinese philosopher Lao Tzu described this beautifully: "If there is to be peace in the world, there must be peace in the nations. If there is to be peace in the nations, there must be peace in the cities. If there is to be peace in the cities, there must be peace between neighbors. If there is to be peace between neighbors, there must be peace in the home. If there is to be peace in the home, there must be peace in the heart." This starts by letting go.

Chapter 4 – Practicing Radical Self-Acceptance

Letting go of past hurts or failures first requires radical self-acceptance in the present. Otherwise we stay trapped regretting our inadequacies or perceiving events as unfair punishments. To cite 12th century Buddhist monk Shinran, "No matter how evil one's past life may be, the light of one thought of taking refuge can wipe it out." What powerful permission to blossom just as we are!

Yet we swim in cultural conditioning that ties self-worth to titles, net worth, appearances and achievements. No wonder even the most outwardly successful people secretly battle feeling inadequate. We instinctively hide our struggles while judging anyone else floundering as weak or unwise. To protect our image, we deny inner turmoil. Thus healing eludes us.

What if peace required fully embracing rather than fixing yourself? Mystics say wholeness comes from befriending our darkness and loving our light equally. Researchers echo similar: self-acceptance directly fuels happiness. The more we argue with reality the more we suffer. All emotions and life stages have their rightful place. As blogger Vironika Tugaleva wrote "Self love is not contingent on circumstances. It's a commitment to myself regardless of emotions, temporary appearances or outside validation."

This commitment to loving ourselves whole initiates our new foundation. Each following chapter then builds tools to forgive others. But self-directed compassion marks the critical start.

The Power of Naming Your Truth

We balk at bringing shadow emotions into the light out of fear of judgment. But words release their grip. Research shows journaling reduces anxiety around vulnerabilities, boosts T-cell production and enrolls the brain's executive functioning for solutions. Begin journaling to voice any self-judgment about perceived flaws, insecurities, embarrassing moments or other truths. This venting ushers the first glimpse of self-compassion. Notice emotions shift from shame and anger to sadness then relief.

After privately airing troubles, share truths that feel safe with non-judgmental friends. Risk going a bit further with each telling. Gather reactions showing most people emphasize far more than you realized. The solution lies not in self-improvement but self-embrace. As psychologist Carl Rogers explained "The curious paradox is that when I accept myself just as I am, then I can change." Judge less. Accept more.

Write a Letter from Your Wise Self

Us critical types tend to listen better when wisdom comes from outside authorities. So imagine your ideal nurturing mentor existed. Draft a letter they would write gently championing all aspects of you. Detail what they love seeing in you. How they interpret shortcomings compassionately through a child's eyes. Affirmations they would share to fan your self-worth. Then read this letter aloud daily as if it were real to override self-attacks.

The Shadow Work Path

More lasting transformation unfolds by thanking our emotions for their lessons. Anger warned against mistreatment. Fear protected. Sadness requested comfort. Shame asked for boundaries. Each has value so embracing the growth opportunity within builds self-trust to heed their messages calmly next time. Nothing requires fixing or hiding.

Therapists use parts mediation to lovingly address emotional conflicts spread across our psyche. You visualize each persona that carries an emotion, life experience or belief as real. Then compassionately learn from them, set boundaries, cultivate teamwork, ask why they act out and what they need to trust you. Results studied show reduced depression, healthy new coping behaviors and feeling internally unified.

In short, radical self acceptance owns all within us so that nothing requires hiding outwardly either. We discover a boundless reserve of grace and guidance flowing through life's messiness perfectly once judgment lifts. What freedom to walk in the world just as we are! Now apply these lessons of compassion onto others too.

Chapter 5 – Understanding Those Who Have Hurt You

Grievances keep us hostage by obscuring why people made choices that caused harm. We assign malicious motives to their actions then condemn them as terrible human beings. But behind all perceived evil lurks profound suffering. Those cleaving to moral high ground actually reveals a lack of empathy. Understanding breeds forgiveness.

The famed poem "Autobiography in Five Chapters" by Portia Nelson illustrates this beautifully: "I walk down the street. There is a deep hole in the sidewalk. I fall in...I am lost ... unable to find a way out. It isn't my fault...It takes forever to find a way out. Chapter Two – I walk down the street. There is a deep hole in the sidewalk. I pretend I don't see it. I fall in again. I can't believe I am in this same place. But, it isn't my fault. It still takes a long time to get out...Chapter Three – I walk down the same street. There is a deep hole in the sidewalk. I see it is there. I fall in ... it's a habit...but, my eyes are open. I know where I am. It is my fault. I get out immediately...Chapter Four – I walk down the same street. There is a deep hole in the sidewalk. I walk around it...Chapter Five – I walk down a different street."

Seeing the humanity in those who once disappointed you similarly allows walking a different path unfettered by past wounds. The key rests in realizing their harmful choices likely aimed to temporarily ease their own suffering – not maliciously target you.

Consider why people lie. Covering up betrayals or mistakes seems morally bankrupt. But probing deeper reveals fear of consequences as the motivator. Similar to how small children fib to avoid punishment, most adults do so hoping to preempt catastrophic outcomes imagined if the truth surfaced. Have compassion for their insecurity and how lying sadly backfires creating more suffering when integrity may have diffused things faster.

Or why do toxic people play the victim, refusing to take responsibility? This outrage glue bonds others to them who buy into the outward victim act. Underneath they likely battle feeling worthless and unlovable. But disempowered tactics for attention never gets core attachment needs met. Have compassion for their agony.

What about dealing with a narcissist unable to empathize with your plight during conflicts? Researchers reveal narcissists suffered chronic emotional neglect as children leaving them unable to connect with their own feelings, much less tune into others. The inflated ego became the fix for regulating a turbulent self image. They didn't choose maladaptive coping tools. But understanding this suffering helps us forgive their limitations.

Even sociopaths and psychopaths share one core commonality: nearly all endured severe childhood trauma. Brain scans show underdeveloped areas controlling empathy and healthy bonding. One study interviewed violent offenders about their earliest memory: repeated themes of molestation, brutality, being locked in closets surfaced. One cannot excuse horrible actions. But seeing the backstory triggers compassion to help end such cycles.

As analyst Jordan Peterson explained "You repair the damage when you understand the cause." This applies inwardly too. Have you avoided examining why past betrayals sting so deeply? Often childhood emotional neglect, attachment losses or not having dependency needs met trains the psyche to expect harm. Current pains then tap into old wounds. Self forgiveness flows from recognizing root origins.

In summary, radical compassion towards those who disappointed you frees resentment's grasp. Allow empathy to soften edges with wisdom. Understanding why people made choices eases anger by unraveling mistaken assumptions. Opening your heart this way builds courage and invites others to let go too. The results can redeem relationships seemingly destroyed.

Chapter 6 – The Gift of Forgiveness

Few acts feel as liberating as forgiving someone who caused harm. Yet paradoxically it also benefits them through renewed connection. Thus forging forgiveness represents a mutual gift nurturing both people and the relationship. It simply starts by shifting from blame to seeking understanding. But how specifically is this done? Let's uncover the methods.

Forgiveness Mantras

Repeating simple phrases helps reframe our mindset and release anger gradually. The calming effects work even if skepticism remains initially. Over time, the words unwind resentment when paired with reflection. Therapists consider mantras highly effective for lessening bitterness from small slights to profound betrayal.

Begin crafting your own sentence starting with "I forgive you for..." to address a specific hurt then add a compassionate reason like "...because carrying resentment only steals my joy." Repeat it silently first thing in the morning and during the day whenever painful memories resurface. Or speak the mantra aloud when safely alone to calm the nervous system.

Another approach uses an all-purpose phrase without specifying an event. Examples include:

- I release this anger and regain my peace.

- That was then, this is now. I choose happiness.

- I wish them well on their journey.

You may doubt the power mantras hold or feel resistant trying it initially. But over time the effects compound just as negatively ruminating creates more bitterness. Mantras interrupt the cycle so true healing can unfold.

Rituals for Letting Go

Ritual harnesses the potent clarity offered through symbolism. Conducting private acts that represent wiping the slate clean provide another way to galvanize forgiveness. Write all lingering hurts and resentments in a letter. Vent fully without holding back, then burn it outdoors. Sprinkle the ashes as a sign of physically releasing the past.

Alternatively, select a rock to represent each major pain caused by someone's actions. One by one, hurl those rocks far into woods or water. Bid goodbye to carrying those heavy burdens as you do. Shake your body loose afterwards to symbolize freedom from negative energy. Ritual grounds us, gives emotions an outlet and consolidates decision making neurologically.

Confront vs Conceding

Forgiveness never implies weakness or surrendering boundaries that prevent repeated harm. We must learn to confront problems head on minus exaggerated emotional reactions. Handling conflicts calmly with honesty about one's feelings proves far more effective for reaching equitable solutions.

True forgiveness acknowledges the fuller humanity of both people in misunderstandings. We label actions as problematic, not the person as fundamentally flawed. This nuance focuses on finding mutual understanding. Sometimes healing conversations uncover ignorance or unintended impacts needing correction. Honest dialogue plants the first seeds of reconciliation which letting go and pardoning actions can ultimately complete later. Confront constructively, then forgive authentically.

The Two Sides of Apologies

When injured, receiving a sincere apology accelerates healing by demonstrating remorse and intention to improve. Rarely does an earnest apology fail to begin thawing hurts within us. Yet even without apologies, we still can forgive. Holding out until offenders bow in repentance keeps you locked in victimhood awaiting their move.

Forgiveness flows from a position of power not needing others' validation. Thus when you're ready to pardon someone still blaming you, first apologize for your own mistakes in the conflict. Admitting how you negatively contributed – even unintentionally – models accountability and invites authentic connection. Then they can accept their wrongs without shame. But lead with humility and self honesty when you've been hurt. It establishes common ground to reconcile from.

When to Walk Away

Forgiving doesn't require further contact or trusting people who repeatedly harm you. In fact, showing grace towards someone from afar often becomes necessary medicine when patterns of broken promises or breaches refusing to stop. We must guard our peace once extended chances expire.

Letting go permits loving others through the lens of basic human dignity without interacting again. It cleans your side of the street fully. Then shifting energy away protects you and allows their journey unfold for ultimate good. Some call this loving people but leaving the relationship. In any case, we release others in love – trusting divine order guides all souls perfectly.

Support Third Party Healing

Interestingly, research on forgiveness revealed that pardoning groups or individuals completely unrelated to one's own grievances still increased life satisfaction, lowered depression and built empathy. This reveals the interconnected nature of healing. World peace literally begins with inner peace.

So after making amends in broken relationships directly, also contemplate sending loving prayers to third parties needing grace. Visualize humanity's classic wounds around betrayal, abandonment and imperfect parents as finally reconciled. Wish abusers and oppressed groups alike freedom from pain driving hurtful choices. See global healing unfolding. Doing so transmutes your newfound liberation into a gift that feeds the world. Then watch forgiveness ripple outwards.

Chapter 7 – Why the Past and Future Rob You of the Present

We human beings love distraction. Endlessly rehashing the past and worrying about the future fills most mental space. Yet neither truly exist beyond memory and imagination. Meanwhile we scarcely notice the present – the only place life actually unfolds! This illusion robs vitality, breeds anxiety and stalls forward movement. Letting go requires residing fully in each moment without obstruction .from what came before or dread of what's next

The brain continually projects you back into past failures or ahead into feared scenarios. Evolutionary advantage explains why. Recalling dangerous events helps avoid future threats. Imagining worst case outcomes supposedly helps preparation too. Our hunter-gatherer ancestors who mastered this survived .and passed down this anticipatory genius

But today this once protective pattern becomes self sabotage. Dwelling on the past cultivates regret, self criticism and victimhood. Obsessing on the future manufactures endless worry, procrastination and analysis paralysis. We scarcely .realize the present slips away - where our real power resides

Each moment brims with open possibilities and fresh choices. When we bring full attention here, life transforms. New perceptions surface. Creativity ignites. People feel your warmth. Doors open synchronistically. This explains why scientists find mindfulness meditation literally alters brain connectivity in just 8 weeks making focus easier. Living present heals the past and secures the future precisely because .conscious choice operates now

The Impact of Past and Future Thinking

Notice your inner dialogue's fixation about what already happened or fantasies around what will happen soon. The noisy mental pinball squanders peace found in the pause between thoughts. No wonder anxiety and depression rates .skyrocket! The present escapes our grip completely

Overthinking the past cultivates regret and self criticism which manifests physically through inflammation, suppressed immunity and even cellular aging. People dwelling on their mistakes display markedly shorter telomeres revealing the toll rumination takes. Forgiveness research confirms that self condemnation and anger about other's wrongs remain two biggest predictors of early mortality. We literally think !ourselves to death

Meanwhile endlessly worrying about tomorrow wisely got labeled as "premeditated misery." Visualizing dire scenarios seems prudent. But Stanford psychologists found that envisioning catastrophic futures actually backfires making .people feel and perform worse! Our evolution betrays us

Clearly the costs of living in memories and projections outweighs supposed benefits. What if ancient spiritual texts and philosophers urging us to live in the now held literally life saving wisdom all along? Your power, peace and performance fully exists here and now alone. Presence pays dividends immediately with more enthusiasm, mental clarity and intuitive flow. Let's start tuning In.

Chapter 8 – Mindfulness & Meditation for Beginners

We hear about mindfulness meditation constantly these days for good reason. Beyond calming benefits, it builds skills for aligning attention with the riches brimming in the present. Think of it as interval training for realigning focus away from unhelpful mental tangents back onto now. Even brief practice sessions compound quickly making it easier to catch your mind escaping then recenter gently without judgement.

Mindfulness simply means paying attention with total awareness to whatever unfolds each moment without strong attachment to any particular aspect. You don't aim to empty the mind. Instead gentle redirection back onto the current experience lets thoughts flow in and out freely. This Infuses everyday activities with a sense of calm fascination and wholeness.

The renowned Jon Kabat-Zinn distilled it beautifully saying mindfulness means "Paying attention in a particular way: on purpose, in the present moment, and non-judgmentally." When absorbed fully doing ordinary things, life feels quite extraordinary!

To begin, choose an activity happening right now using all five senses. Maybe drinking tea or walking outside. Tune into flavors, sounds, smells, temperature and visual beauty with childlike curiosity. When the mind inevitably wanders, guide it softly back to sensual input flooding before you right now. Thoughts about 5 minutes ago or 10 minutes ahead get gently labeled "remembering" or "planning" before redirecting back.

Start attempts short. Even 5 minutes daily builds mental muscle memory. Be compassionate with lapses and patient growing this skill. Over time, you'll access the refreshing fountain of vitality, creativity and connectivity running through the eternal now with more ease. And symptoms of anxiety, Indignation and lethargy resulting from past/future obsession lift.

As mathematician and philosopher Alain de Botton writes "It's one of the disasters of modern life that we have prioritized speed efficiency and destinations over journeys and getting happily waylaid by the chance offerings of any given hour." Carve out deliberate spaces daily to get gloriously lost appreciating here and now.

Chapter 9 – Appreciating Today, Letting Each Moment Be Enough

Have you ever met someone radiating joy and marveled at their enduring smile despite life's ups and downs? Such individuals ooze gratitude, presence and contentment in simplicity. It turns out appreciation remains the key that unlocks lasting happiness by transforming how we experience reality itself. Fortunately it proves very trainable too.

Watch a young child enthralled smelling flowers, giggling at bubbles or enchanted petting animals. Young children glory in the present, finding delight everywhere through unfiltered senses. Their joy bubbles up seeing basic beauty surrounding them at all times. It has nothing to do with achievements, money or other adult metrics we chase. This youthful wonder lives on inside us all but sometimes requires coaxing back out again.

Studies confirm that actively appreciating present moments creates more positive emotions than focusing on past nostalgia or even optimism about the future! Why? It directs focus onto the riches here now rather than constructing happiness contingently through attainments. We access fulfillment immediately on demand. It turns out we already have so much in our world worthy of feeling gratitude.

Begin practicing radical appreciation for current moments. Use the five senses to notice uncelebrated details going overlooked. Savor flavors and aromas of foods you normally rush through eating. Admire colors, textures and contours in nature close up. Feel pleasant sensations like warmth, a cool breeze, clothing on .skin. Listen intently to sounds alive in that very second

The tiniest aspects suddenly seem wondrous! Our mindset colors reality itself. As researcher Ellen Langer discovered "Notice anything and appreciate it and you'll expand your world because it will expand your mind." Your best life literally waits for you the moment you unfold appreciation's wings .embracing the fullness found here now

Chapter 10 – Tuning Out Distractions About the Past and Future

———

We now understand the heavy toll of overthinking the past and future. Plus mindfulness primes us to anchor Into the present moment as our new home base. Yet old mental habits die hard. Despite best intentions, you'll inevitably catch your mind drifting into reliving history or spinning imaginary scenarios. How exactly then do we catch and correct unhelpful mental tangents? The key rests in building self awareness.

Noticing Thought Patterns

Your inner voice seems to operate on autopilot beyond conscious control. One study found people spend nearly 50% of their waking hours lost in thought! But suddenly noticing thought patterns proves the first step in dismantling distraction.

Here's the exciting news according to Harvard researchers – mind wandering includes rhythms. Your brain alternates between being present focused, then distraction prone, back again predictably every 90 to 120 seconds. Realizing your attention reliably fades then snaps back actually makes catching it easier!

Look for these common hooks that signal your mind drifting:

Reliving Past Events

Replaying conversations -

Regretting mistakes -

Feeling nostalgic -

Worrying About Future

Making predictions -

Envisioning rejections -

Catastrophizing outcomes -

Mental Fantasy

Imagining idealized success -

Revenge or justice fantasies -

Romanticizing people/situations -

Planning/Problem-Solving

Analyzing solutions -

Making strategically decisions -

Judging circumstances -

Again, all these thought patterns prove normal and healthy occasionally. But losing hours obsessively projecting elsewhere robs vitality and life satisfaction. Each time you catch your mind doing this, gently guide focus back to the physical senses. The sights, textures, smells and sounds flooding the here and now.

More Tips For Staying Present

Beyond monitoring thought patterns, supplementary tactics strengthen anchoring into the now:

Label Thoughts

Attach objective descriptors like "planning" "judging" "fantasizing" to pull back.

Set Reminders

Use timers, apps or wrist snaps to remind tuning in.

Single Task

Avoid mentally scattering by giving full attention to one activity.

Limit Input

Cut unnecessary media noise breeding distraction.

Reward Noticing

Celebrate catching your mind wandering as mental muscle memory.

Walk Mindfully

Use natural movement to reign attention inward.

Focus On Senses

?What textures/sights/sounds can you appreciate right here

The Present Moment Portal

Dwelling too much in analysis of why your mind escapes the now proves yet another distraction! Instead of judging habits, simply begin nudging attention continually back onto immediate sensory experiences flooding by. Radical appreciation grows each time present moment awareness gets .rediscovered

Soon you'll move through days with enhanced satisfaction plus consistency staying immersed In here-now reality. Past regrets and future worries then lose their negative charge. Everything required for your best life overflows abundantly right here, !right now

Chapter 11: The Power of Now for Living Your Best Life

The present moment contains everything you need to live a beautiful, fulfilling life. Unfortunately, we habitually close this gateway to peace and joy by mentally residing in the past or future. What possibilities open up by continually returning to and ultimately abiding in the eternal now? Let's explore.

Full Engagement Supercharges Experience

Have you noticed certain pleasant activities like conversations, meals or even working deeply in flow state feel richer, more meaningful and seem to last longer when fully engaged without distraction? Researchers confirm being immersed in the present moment does expand subjective time perception and boosts enjoyment.

In one study, people asked to be highly attentive viewing nature photos later reported the images lasted longer and brought more fulfillment than those casually glimpsing the same pictures multi-tasking. Single tasking with total absorption literally upgrades ordinary events into experiences eliciting awe. Who wouldn't crave more of those peak moments life offers?

Intuition and Insights Increase

Brilliant ideas rarely arrive overthinking things. Flashes of creative insights dawn when relaxing into each moment receptively. Intuition works similarly – you hear its whispering guidance clearly when aligned fully with the now.

Have you noticed how often solutions to problems popup spontaneously in the shower, driving, exercising or waking up? By not striving intellectually, fresh perspectives creep through the back channels of our subconscious. The now brims with inspiration if we patiently receive.

Fulfillment Hides in Plain Sight

Could contentment hide in simplest aspects of normal life instead of distant goals achieved? Those living for tomorrow often feel unhappy despite incredible success. But even carrying groceries, laughing with friends or seeing sunlight through leaves fills ordinary moments with extraordinary beauty when engaged completely.

Presence uncovers the extraordinary within the ordinary. Perhaps life offers delightful secrets for those whispering its language – paying attention. See what unfolds for you by continually returning presence to the now.

The Refreshing Fountain of Now

Have you ever felt mentally exhausted by too much busyness, only to then feel replenished going for a long walk in nature, gazing at the ocean or playing with a child? Just like our body, our distracted minds require immersive pleasures that hit the reset button too.

Make inhabiting the now for even 10-15 minutes daily your mental sanctuary for stress relief, fuzzy thinkers drain and energy renewal. Keep redirecting focus away from analyzation back onto sensations and emotions unfolding right here, right now.

Soon you'll realize the present contains everything needed for living well – creativity, connections, inspiration, peace. Past and future then assume proper proportion instead of distorting reality. Return continually to the power of now until finally residing here effortlessly.

Chapter 12: How Fear and Worry Hold You Back

Mark Twain once quipped "I've had a lot of worries in my life, most of which never happened." Yet we spend incredible energy anxiously obsessing over what might go wrong. Is all this worrying worthwhile or actually counterproductive? Let's explore what science reveals.

The Purpose of Worry

Worry seems helpful for avoiding problems by preparing for worst case outcomes. Our early ancestors who anticipated threats supposedly survived more often, passing down this tendency genetically. Today, academics still contend moderate worrying aids goal achievement and pre-empts dangers ahead.

But new research using brain Imaging dispels many myths about worry's usefulness:

Worriers display distorted threat perception. Non-worriers more accurately judge risk likelihood using facts appropriately balanced with intuition for reasonable preparation. But worriers blow possibilities out of proportion while ignoring probability context.

The act of worrying rarely sparks productive solutions. - Thinking sessions focused on analyzing action plans directly proves much more effective for coming up with ideas to mitigate risks. Worrying tends to spiral circularly rehashing the .same fears rather than moving towards answers

WORRYING CORRELATES to worse, not better - performance. Envisioning future failures often becomes a self-fulfilling prophecy. Stanford psychologists found that visualizing worst case scenarios Increased anxiety which caused worse outcomes later. Apparently evolution betrayed us with .this leftover habit

People cannot successfully multi-task worrying and working - simultaneously. Attempting to tackles life duties while spinning internal panic steals bandwidth draining effectiveness. It explains why anxious individuals suffer twice .the rates of Impaired productivity

CLEARLY WORRY FAILS to deliver practical advantages modern society assumes. But breaking free requires understanding the psychology underpinning this wasteful .mental habit

Why We Worry

If worry sabotages functioning, why do most people still obsessively indulge in it? The answers trace back to our deepest ...human needs

The sense of control – Uncertainty triggers feelings of helplessness igniting our need to self soothe. Worrying satisfies ego's illusion that we can shape all outcomes. Of course, this remains pure fantasy, but to anxious minds brings comfort.

Seeking meaning – Assigning significance to events makes life feel less random which we interpret as safer at core. Even framing adversity as punishment for personal defects or test from the universe holds deeper appeal than considering circumstances meaningless chance.

Validating existence – Having an active Internal world focused on ourselves, even negatively, helps combat unconscious existential dread. Silencing those worried inner voices risks confronting emptiness. So we buffer the void by keeping narratives of impending disasters occupying awareness.

Avoidance coping – Rehashing all possible troubles ahead defends against mourning losses or past emotional injuries in the present. Keeping our mind locked in forward panic denies feeling sadness, anger or regret in lieu of obsessive worry.

In summary, worry serves key psychological functions. But manifests as distorted perceptions about reality and breeds catastrophic thinking cycles generating unnecessary suffering. Time to unravel this habit...

Chapter 13: Releasing Anxious Thoughts and Embracing Calm

As an anxious child, Emma constantly imagined worst case scenarios happening to her loved ones. Vivid nightmares of accidents or her house burning left her distraught each morning. As a working mom, Emma's worrying compulsively focused on her young son now too. Obsessively plotting out his days to minimize any risk, she controlled his playmates and after school activities without even realizing it. This worrying felt like love – securing his safety above all else.

Of course, anxiety disorders commonly disguise as vigilance. Emma believed her habit of envisioning danger prepared them better. That was until the sleepless nights, chronic headaches and panic attacks worried her instead. She realized anxiety stole quality of life rather than securing it. Emma began seeking tools to break free from the grip of worry for good. Let's look at what finally started working:

Catch Unhelpful Thinking

Psychologists reveal several distorted thought patterns fueling anxiety. Noticing these sneaky mental habits in yourself makes space for logic to intervene:

- Catastrophizing – Imagining the absolute worst case scenario and its impact rather than looking at all potential outcomes together. Ex. A headache means definitely having a brain tumor rather than one of many causes.

- Fortune-telling – Arbitrarily predicting dire futures without considering other variables. Ex. Just because I felt embarrassed before means I won't get the job.

- Emotional reasoning – Assuming your fearful emotions perfectly reflect reality vs potential distortions. Ex. I feel scared about this, so it must be dangerous.

- Perfectionism – Rigid black & white thinking puts unrealistic standards onto life forcing disappointment. Ex. If I'm not 100% prepared, then I will completely fail.

CATCHING HERSELF BLOWING worst case scenarios out of proportion, using fear to predict futures and requiring perfect conditions before feeling safe, Emma began interrupting spiraling thoughts. Just noticing is the first victory. You create mental space seeing the hamster wheel for what it is – a trick of the mind.

Get Back into the Body

When anxiously projecting ahead, we exit the present moment physically too – our only place of power. The brain goes on sensory lockdown neglecting the calming effects of touch, sound, sight, taste. But studies show even brief interludes focusing on the body balances hormones, lowers blood pressure and flips fight-flight back to grounded presence.

Emma used the following techniques to immediately shift worries into bodily tranquility:

5 Sense Check-In – Pause and bring total attention onto objects around you appealing to each sensory channel one at a time. Ex. Feel the shoes on your feet, listen closely to birds chirping, sniff a cup of tea, etc. Even 30 seconds of immersive sensory connection drops anxiety markedly.

Walk Mindfully – Go on short, slow walks without any goal besides witnessing the body moving through space noticing feelings, sounds and scenery happening step by step. Stay out of thoughts by continually redirecting attention to physical sensations.

Body Scans – Lie down attending carefully to physical and emotional feelings in one body region at a time moving progressively from toes to head. This releases mental fixation while deeply relaxing.

Just Breathe – Whenever worries spiral, take 60 seconds focusing solely on the sensation of air filling your chest expanding on the inhale and gradually leaving on the exhale. Say "alert mind, calm body" silently as a mantra while breathing.

These quick tools snap Emma out of hypothetical worries back into the safety of her capable body in the here and now. Give them a try next time anxiety creeps up!

Learn to Tolerate Uncertainty

The true antidote for anxiety lies In building tolerance for uncertainty. Because the unknown trIggers alarms in our brain screaming "danger ahead!" Worriers crave assurances, guarantees, perfect plans and total control to secure safety. But life offers none of that. Disorder remains the natural state of existence. Things change unpredictably and outcomes stay unclear. What we mistake as certainty actually manifests as fluid probabilities and best guesses.

Trying to eliminate uncertainty gets exhausting and impossible. But increasing capacity to bear not knowing brings freedom. Emma practiced ways to gently lean into cloudy futures with curiosity instead of needing to control everything.

Refocus on What You Can Control

When Emma found herself spiraling about her son's wellbeing, she shifted attention back to her own choices. What healthy food can I pack in his lunch today? How will I model self-care habits for him to see? Teaching him the name of every tree in our yard engages him with nature. I'll sign us up for swim lessons together. Loving action feels empowering.

Get Curious About the Unknown

Instead of defaulting to worst case images, Emma practiced asking "I wonder what surprises life might bring?" about uncertain situations. Using imagination to explore possibilities widely opens perspectives beyond just disasters. It turns out optimism relies on considering positive potentials too.

Do a Reality Check

When anxieties mount, assess with logic. Realistically what odds does this bad outcome have - 1% or 40%? Are my imagined catastrophic results exaggerated? How likely is my cat going missing forever because a door was left open? Does getting nervous prevent accidents or does skilled preparation have more impact? Run scenarios by levelheaded friends to reality test proportion.

Challenge Black & White Thinking

Rigid perfectionism requires that either everything goes exactly according to plan or total catastrophe. Shades of grey remain intolerable. But in reality, setbacks mean new openings arise. Emotionally strong people roll with disappointments by creatively adapting. Reframe worries into neutral challenges to grow through.

Let Go of Needing to Know

Research at UC Berkeley found that intolerance of uncertainty directly correlates to anxiety levels. The drive for absolute guarantee against negatives ironically fuels panic. But releasing attachment to perfect assurance opens you to possibilities. Survey history and notice how often things work out given time, even if difficult at first. Have faITh in beneficial unfoldment.

By learning to lean into cloudy outcomes curiously, while controlling only her responsive choices, Emma short-circuited chronic worry patterns. She discovered anxiety relaxes when .trusting life's unfolding design

Reframe Worries Into Problem-Solving Mode

Of course avoiding real threats remains essential for functioning. The key becomes distinguishing solvable concerns from useless hypothetical worrying that steals joy. Once Emma determined a fear held realistic validity, she pivoted focus onto .pragmatic solutions

For example, worrying about having enough savings in case of emergency held merit. Rather than spin scenarios about ending up broke and homeless, Emma made a plan. She set up automatic monthly transfers into a savings account. Feeling in .control of wise preparation calmed money worries

Psychologists say focusing mental energy on secondary problems generated by a primary concern proves unproductive. People don't realize harboring anger that a bad event happened won't make the event itself better. The constructive approach involves asking "What step can I take next?" Contingency .planning relieves anxiety and builds confidence

Reframe Fear Into Excitement

Studies confirm it's physiologically impossible to experience excitement and anxiety simultaneously. Both show nearly identical body symptoms like racing heart, sweaty palms, adrenaline surge. The sole difference lies in mental framing alone.

Fearful worriers interpret those sensations negatively as signs of danger. But adventurers frame the same internal experiences as excitement! This life-changing hack allows flipping common anxieties into eager energy.

Emma found visualizing worries as thrillIng adventures needing courage changed everything. Public speaking seemed less intimidating reframed as the thrill of connecting with people through stories. New challenges got embraced as exciting unknowns to grow through rather than threats.

Go have some fun with It! Which of your worries transform Into joyful anticipatory excitement just by shifting perspective? This approach can turn panic into playfulness about life's plot twist up ahead !

Chapter 14: Having Faith That Things Will Work Out

Former professional basketball player Kevin Durant once said "Have faith. No matter how chaotic it is right now, everything will work itself out." Easier said than done for chronic worriers though! Having faith requires relinquishing two key illusions: that past experience perfectly predicts futures and that you somehow control external outcomes. What positive psychology tells us about building this empowering mind shift?

Get Out of the Predictive Brain

Brains evolved primarily for threat detection – to envision negative futures effectively avoiding harm. Our ancestors who excelled at pattern recognition steered clear of past dangers securing survival legacy. So modern minds (wrongly) assume if something went wrong before, we must worry to avoid repeats.

Of course, sometimes risks reoccur. But probability theory confirms both bad and good events rarely happen consistently by sheer chance alone. Just because you got the flu last year doesn't determine virus exposure this season. Yet worriers fall victim to distortion bias assuming past losses dictate future failures.

Faithful thinkers know millions of variables impact results moment to moment. So while considering past troubles has merit for preparation, worrying about repeats wastes energy. We must transcend obsolete programming that yesterday perfectly predicts tomorrow. Each day unfolds 100% new.

The Illusion of Control

Our egos crave influence over external realities far exceeding actual capacities. We seek guarantees by micromanaging environments, people and outcomes around an illusion of control. Without conscious awareness anxiously controlling behavior disguises fearful doubts about trustworthiness of life's flow overall.

Yet deep wisdom traditions teach surrendering rather than grasping tight actually allows life to bless you. Letting go and acknowledging mystery opens unseen potentials. Consider windswept palm trees during storms... they survive violent weather by flowing flexible not rigidly resisting. The tallest oak trees snap against fierce winds while palms fluidly bend without breaking.

Releasing the exhausting illusion of forcing outcomes builds faith in forces larger than self directing all things. Adopting beginner's mind helps too – perceiving life's uncertainties as a curious explorer. "I wonder how this will unfold?" begins opening probabilities with patience. Go with the flow.

Growth Opportunities Hide Behind Setbacks

Self help author Napoleon Hill famously attested that "every adversity carries with it the seed of an equivalent or greater benefit." Look closely at perceived failures and suddenly lessons emerge.

Losing a job led Marie to blossom into extensive creativity pursuits she lacked time for before. Ending toxic relational dynamics freed Kate's energy to finally achieve fitness goals. Missing a flight led Jake to meet his future wife charmingly at the airport lounge. The bless-in-disguise gets revealed later but first requires planting faith seeds.

Cultivating Capital Mindset

Entrepreneurial thought leader, Erik Finman, acknowledges market downturns and other systemic disruptions require preservation. But instead of worrying what may happen next he chooses to remain steadfast envisioning capital building after storms pass.

This "capital mindset" focuses on controlling only the controllable – working diligently, skilling up, conserving money. Worrying just zaps bandwidth diminishing responsive power. A long term positive vision pulls people through troubles better than reacting fears.

Faith proves self fulfilling – confidence creates capable thoughts and actions manifesting strength which builds more faith iteratively. Watch how even tiny seeds of believing challenges hide opportunities cultivates empowerment. Suddenly you don't just survive but thrive through turbulence.

Reframing Victim Stories

Resilience gurus reference two prime stories we subconsciously believe dictating how we frame reality's upsets: victim narrative and growth narrative. Seeing bad events as punishments 'done to you' breeds helplessness. But viewing trials as growth lessons for developing grit keeps agency alive.

Catch internal self talk after getting passed up for promotion, fights with friends or car breakdowns. Do you cast the universe as villain sabotaging you? Or use setback to uncover blind spots needing worked on? Flip feelings of unfairness into opportunity mentality and notice faith arise in time as blessing reveal themselves.

Cultivating Trust Through Uncertainty

Since worry aims to secure safety, building radical trust In life's uncertainties can seem counterintuitive at first. But the same chaos worrying tries to eliminate actually contains order when viewed through a wider lens. This faith rests In embracing reality as essentially "good" unfolding optimally.

Research shows that welcoming all circumstances without resisting unwanted aspects trains the brain to expect favorable resolutions naturally. You develop tolerance for short term ambiguity, knowing things ultimately work out given time.

Practicing affirmations like "I am safe, life supports me" while envisioning goodwill inherent everywhere combats reflexive doubt. Seeing interconnection of all things and people as Divinely orchestrated dissipates fear of Isolation during trials.

Additionally, focusing on "what is" instead of "what ifs" grounds the mind in factual reality not dreadful imagination. Deal with troubles when they actually manifest, not spun worries that rarely arrive. Stay present.

Finally, list previous examples in your life when difficulties passed and things improved unexpectedly. Recall moments when generosity or compassion blessed your day amidst sadness. This builds neural evidence that goodness exists waiting to crystallize despite temporary troubles. Have faith in unseen forces guiding your path.

Surrender Control, Embrace Mysteries

Releasing need for control requires embracing uncertanties as essential mysteries instead of threats. Dark nights hide the very seeds necessary for glorious sunrises.

Consider the Japanese art of Kintsugi - repairing broken pottery using liquid gold to seal cracks with special beauty. They symbolize how vessels once shattered can become even more unique and valuable welded carefully back together. The philosophy applies to life's heartbreaks too - gold awaits undiscovered from proper mending.

Or reflect on carbon's properties... when pressurized slowly over eons inside rocky wombs, it transforms Into diamonds! Dull chunks of black coal contain secret potential to crystallize into the world's most brilliant gems given the right (albeit arduous) conditions.

Your current doubts and troubles likely disguise untapped gifts awaiting activation through patient faith during difficulty. Trust in eventual value emerging through life's messiness. .Worry less, wonder more

Chapter 15: Allowing Life to Unfold Without Trying to Control Everything

Attempting to dominate life's uncertainties not only proves exhausting but counterproductive. The sheer effort of continually fighting for the illusion of control steals energy that might get invested into growth opportunities disguised within the turmoil we dread. What if embracing, not resisting is the secret to simultaneously reducing worry and accessing peace?

The Costs of Chronic Control

Perfectionists and chronic worriers share common tendencies – requiring flawless conditions to feel safe while believing they single handedly ensure security vigilantly managing the variables. If anything remains uncertain or beyond influence, anxiety sounds internal alarms forecasting pending disasters.

Of course a degree of control over little details grants functioning. But the obsessive hyper-focus exaggerates your actual sphere of influence. Watch close and see how trying to control life forcefully fails:

- PEOPLE REMAIN FREE agents who won't be manipulated or controlled long term.

- Forcing outcomes builds rigidity blinding you to solutions arising unexpectedly.

- The universe unfolds as it will anyway despite your attempts of domination.

- Holding on tightly to anything guarantees loss, while allowing cultivates flow.

So why do we chronically overlook reality's built in uncertainties out of ego's fantasy of directing externals? And is peace possible while surrendering need for assurance?

The Psychology of Control

Seeking excessive control disguises underlying fears about lacking safety at core. Like gasping harder when oxygen runs low, ego grasps desperately trying to eradicate feelings of danger when life feels out of hand.

Of course no amount of straining changes external conditions. But to anxious minds relief comes pretending some small domain can get mastered, numbing awareness of the surrounding wildness waiting. We constrict the entire world into bite sized pieces digestible for our fears.

When big picture anxieties seem intolerable, we narrow focus on things seeming "doable" – cleaning, planning, structuring habits. Constructively organizing details isn't the issue. The trouble arises denying the inherent messiness frame by frame trying to clean life's unruly canvas completely.

By acknowledging the world's beautiful chaos exceeding humankind's capacities, but engaging responsibly anyway, worry abates. Control dissolves as illusion while personal agency gets restored. How exactly is this embodied?

Cultivate Mastery, Surrender Attachments

Navy seals undergoing harsh survival training adopt mantra "Calm, Cool, Collected" when physical and mental breakdown threatens mission failure. Paradoxically stressed officers transcend panic only when releasing desperate grasping for Dominion over extreme conditions. Resilience lives in the space between scrambling for control and helpless floating adrift.

Masterful living works similarly – fully committing to excel at whatever gets undertaken with passionate energy while surrendering attachment to perfect outcomes. Be responsibly empowered but emotionally flexible simultaneously. Growth depends not on error proofing life forcefully but flowing iteratively with results unfolding.

We suffer terribly from arguing with and resisting realities as they manifest. Anxiety about unwanted aspects strangles enjoyment of available blessings before our eyes right now. Like the executive coaching adage goes "You can have it all, just not all at once." Take the sequential path and trust life's artistry.

Make Friends With Uncertainty

Releasing need for assurance every step ahead contradicts societal messaging that living strategically promises satisfaction. But cold logic fails to predict realities replete with wonderful surprises both for better and worse.

Ancient wisdom traditions contend the very unpredictability of life unites people in shared vulnerability beyond concepts inventing separate status. And hinted that befriending rather than battling uncertainty held the ultimate secret to peace within.

Modern behavioral research confirms anxiety disorders strongly correlate with intolerance of uncertainty. The drive for total assurance ironically fuels panic. But releasing need for fixed clarity and guarantees allows greater trust in organically unfolding outcomes. Progress depends not on predicting every detail but persisting through murky periods with resilient hope.

Moreover, scientists find randomness itself contains amazing self organizing properties when unmanipulated. Consider how impossibly enmeshed ecosystems balance largely by magic without micromanagement. Or gaps in conversation invite unexpected insights to emerge. Appreciate uncertainty's gifts!

Focus On Yourself, Not Others

Attempts at nagging people into better behavior or envisioning exactly how scenarios should play out turn sour fast. Attachment to perfect fantasy breeds bitterness when reality diverges. And shame people when their actions don't mirror your ideals.

The constructive approach involves minding your business! Effect change through modeling not mandate. Stay focused on refining your output without worrying whether hearts and minds align out there. With clear priorities, you can allow others' journey unfold while creating ripples through standing as inspiring example. Detach from needing specific reactions.

Let people miss the memo initially. Trust wisdom gets embedded in those meant to receive it even if timelines seem delayed. Consider the Japanese proverb "Arrows that hit the right spots can penetrate even rock." Your work reaches the destined. Release timetables and keep envisioning highest aims realized.

Catch Yourself Strategizing

Finally, notice urges to seize command of circumstances. Observe how quickly mind races to "figure things out" when discomfort arises from not knowing, mistakes happen, or people don't comply. Vertical analysis temporarily substitutes for vulnerable feelings threatening.

Catch mental wiring escaping present moment awareness through obsessive planning about the past or future. Gently invite identification back into the safety of body and breath. Then widen perspective acknowledging you participate co-creatively with variables exceeding anyone's solo control. Ride the interactive field together.

Through opening to receive life's uncertain unfolding while responsibly tending your corner of the garden, worry subsides. Control dissolves as illusion while personal freedom expands exponentially. Get out of your own way so everything can find its way to you!

Rosa loved growing orchids. She cultivated 50 vibrant plants in her backyard greenhouse, each unique species bearing delicate blooms in rare colors and designs. The flowers uplifted Rosa's loneliness since her beloved husband passed away. She invested immense time researching caretaking techniques to nourish .their finicky needs

Mastering proper temperature, moisture, fertilization and greenhouse air flow kept the orchids healthy for decades...until suddenly disease struck. Flowers wilted, leaves spotted. No matter how Rosa scrambled adjusting techniques, within .months over 80% of her treasured collection perished

Rosa obsessed for hours plotting to sterile the remaining plants. As she disinfected the greenhouse again weeping in frustration, old Clara, the neighborhood oak tree, whispered .wisdom through the window

Clara assured Rosa that her orchids thrived so abundantly precisely because of the tender love poured Into them daily. However in quiet moments, wasn't It obvious that elements like weather and microbial fluctuations exceeding Rosa's ?control also influenced the greenhouse environment

As cruel mystery as it seemed, perhaps the orchid plague invited Rosa into deep acceptance of life's uncertainty after years hiding busily behind proud self-reliance since widowhood. All things change and perish, even cherished loves. Letting go allows make space for the new. Fighting reality .only delays healing

Rosa sighed acknowledging the truth. She lovingly composted the decaying orchids to nourish the soil. She rinsed and dried the green housing, removing imperfection temptation remnants. Then Rosa rested watching the sun set In trust that a
.new dawn would soon emerge

The next morning just before sunrise, Rosa gasped witnessing an unexpected sight – rather than decay, one majestic orchid had climbed from compost achieving dazzling bloom! It's resplendent colors and sweet aroma blessed Rosa with hope. Clara rustled proudly sharing finally it was not Rosa's forceful
.schemes that ever grew gorgeous orchids

Instead, when Rosa surrendered needing outcomes her way, space opened for Life's hidden wisdom to surprise her with even more abundant gifts than imaginable alone. The orchid's transcendent beauty today could only arrive because Rosa finally trusted the light again even in the darkness. From now, she would nurture plants attentively but without attachment to
.expectations

Chapter 16: Setting Healthy Boundaries

Forgiving past hurts or overcoming worry about the future represents huge personal growth. However, achieving long-term serenity requires establishing healthy boundaries with people and situations moving forward. Otherwise well-meaning folks may continue impacting your equilibrium without realizing it. Or you regress falling into old co-dependent caretaking habits out of guilt. What exactly are boundaries and how are they created?

Defining Your Boundaries

At essence, boundaries represent defined physical, mental and emotional limits denoting where you end and others begin – distinguishing needs, responsibilities and burdens alike. People lacking boundaries feel drained enabling others' dysfunction or seem quick taking offenses personally. Learning to self-regulate empowers you to choose consciously how to respond despite external triggers.

Common areas requiring boundaries:

Physical – Protecting personal space, sexuality, belongings, privacy, etc

Time/Energy – Determining how much gets invested into various relationships or activities day to day

Caretaking – Stepping back from excessive responsibility for others' choices and emotions

Values – Enforcing aligned morals and integrity rather than compromising for acceptance

Psychological Triggers – Managing emotional flashbacks like abuse or neglect that replay during stress

Nearly everyone grew up lacking sufficient modeling around boundaries from caretakers. But thankfully they prove teachable through simple daily practice. You must define limits before expecting anyone to respect them though. So where specifically do you feel compromised?

How to Set Boundaries Gracefully

Effectively communicating boundaries without attacking others' character involves owning your experiences by using "I statements". For example with a narcissistic parent:

"I feel belittled when you insult my career choices. I need encouragement, not shame from you. I will walk away the next time that happens to take care of myself."

With a friend who texts excessively:

"I care deeply for you yet feel overwhelmed trying to instantly reply to so many messages daily. I will respond meaningfully a few times per week instead so we can both stay focused."

Use language emphasizing respect for the relationship alongside requiring consent going forward. Be clear on wants versus mandates. Explain impacts of behaviors without accusations. Offer alternatives that meet mutual needs gracefully.

What does successfully holding boundaries look like day to day? You calmly enforce your stated limits through actions without needing apologies or changed hearts first. Walk away mid conversation with those steamrolling. Counter mistruths about you directly without expecting mea culpas. Graciously decline favors if strings attached. Disconnect briefly when repeatedly disrespected.

The model Mahatma Gandhi described beautifully rings true: "Nonviolence requires a double faith – faith in God and faith in man." Have courage voicing your reality while trusting Life's intelligence directing all beings. Now let's build discernment around codependency relapse risk situations sinking your serenity unconsciously...

Common Boundary Pitfalls

Do these scenarios trigger you abandoning healthy limits again out of guilt, people pleasing Orin hoots of lingering inadequacy?

- Helping others at your own expense self sacrificially

- Over functioning trying to "fix" other's poor choices

- Staying in unhealthy relationships hoping they'll finally change

- Doubting self worth without external validation

- Enduring mistreatment to be seen as "good person"

Regressing into weak boundaries happens slowly like the classic frog parable...If you toss a frog into boiling water it immediately jumps out. But if you increase temperature slowly, it complacently boils to death unnoticing.

Similarly when exhausted, stressed or craving acceptance you may allow poor treatment creeping back in a little at a time eroding boundaries unconsciously. "I'll just answer this one midnight call even though we agreed I would keep phone off overnight for self care." "I'll help surprise visit my lonely dad even though it ruins my plans."

Watch for waivering boundaries early before serious relapse cascades and gently recommit to soul-aligned limits without self shaming. Celebrate tiny daily progress. Enlist supportive friends to validate choices. With consistent practice holding boundaries gets easier until you finally default into healthy alignment automatically. Homeostasis arises as the new normal. Maintain serenity with sustained mindfulness. Mastering the art of boundaries grants freedom to then authentically...

When Others Resist Your Boundaries:

It's quite common for people accustomed to controlling you, exploiting your time or depending on your emotional labor to resist newly established boundaries. Some may lash out angrily at suddenly denied privileges or feel abandoned by your distance.

Narcissists especially may aggressively threaten or devalue you for daring to not comply with their demands. Stand firm expecting pushback, but don't justify the validity of your needs to anyone. Disengage debate attempts completely by broken records reiterating the boundary itself.

"I understand this change feels frustrating. I hold firm to only being available by phone on weekends as I stated, in order to take care of my health."

Broken records persist without explaining further or reacting emotionally. Narcissists crave divisive reactions to create drama—deny this 'narcissistic supply'. They eventually tire moving on once your steady boundary stops fueling attention needs.

Additionally, when others disrespect stated boundaries, immediate enactment without waiting or reminding them proves essential. Don't issue idle threats hoping behavior improves eventually without follow through action. Demonstrate you mean business by walking away mid conversation, declining favors, or restricting access in the moment. Although uncomfortable initially, consistency training people how you allow yourself to be treated bears fruit later establishing long term harmony once boundaries get respected.

When You Mess Up Boundaries:

Despite best intentions, you will slip up occasionally failing to enforce stated limits in the heat of conflict or emotional hijacks blinding your judgment. Perfection can't be expected overnight after a lifetime missing boundary modeling and practice.

During lapses don't spiral shame and self criticism leading to abandonment of retraining altogether as 'impossible'. All growth comes through iteration. Apologize to yourself first, then clean up impacts of temporary slips with others graciously. Quickly resume boundary practicing instead of fixating faults.

Perhaps communicate "I allowed my boundary around taking work calls after 8pm to be pushed last night inexcusably. I apologize if the late hour affected you, while I work to reinforce firm time limits looking ahead." Then refocus proudly back onto priority of self care. Over time unconsciously dismissive habits get replaced with intentional empowerment no matter what occurred yesterday. Progress over perfection!

Lindsey's Struggle with People-Pleasing

Lindsey always struggled saying no, perpetually putting others' wants before her own needs. She resented feeling spread thin accommodating endless favors, but guilt and "good girl" conditioning kept the cycle spinning.

In college, Lindsey regularly skipped meals and sleep trying to tutor flailing classmates who often didn't even show up. At her corporate job, Lindsey stayed late routinely, anxiety magnifying about unfinished reports. Yet her work-life balance dissolved.

The pattern climaxed when Lindsey's BFF, Jane, asked an exhausting request – could Jane stay for 6 whole months at Lindsey's downtown condo for free while restarting her career post-divorce? Lindsey cringed imagining relinquishing her treasured personal space in definitively. Heart racing, she knew refusing felt terrifying yet necessary for the first time.

Mustering courage, Lindsey somehow stammered "Actually, I can only host short term. My condo doesn't allow long term guests per the lease." Jane looked confused having never heard Lindsey set limits before. Didn't "besties do anything" for each other?

Lindsey stood firm reiterating "I'm happy to help you transition but can only offer my place for one month." Later privately, she sent Jane affordable rental listings too.

Jane grumbled at the denial but soon found arrangements. After moving out however, Jane began ghosting Lindsey suddenly. Lindsey felt crushed wondering if the rare boundary attempt cost their decade long friendship permanently? Yet Lindsey also noticed less resentment towards Jane these days without continuing co-dependent enmeshing.

Soon Lindsey decided more allies supporting her evolving strength mattered most, not clinging onto those benefiting from her past weaknesses. She joined empowerment workshops on boundaries and self-care. Incrementally saying no came easier without dreadful guilt churning within.

Months later Jane finally resurfaced asking to meet. She shared tearfully "I was so upset initially when you set that boundary declining my lengthy stay. It highlighted how I had taken advantage of your generosity for years actually. I needed time self reflecting because I wasn't being a supportive friend at all. But I've changed and want to show up for you better now if you'll have me again."

Lindsey smiled extending forgiveness while also acknowledging both women required establishing healthy mutual limits moving forward. No longer entangled anxiously, their friendship blossomed beautifully instead. Lindsey walked taller having learned she could prioritize needs without sabotaging relationships or abandoning people. Her world expanded once those suffocating people pleasing pressures lifted.

Sometimes the hardest boundaries become the most liberating long term even when initially challenging social conditioning. Have courage speaking loving truth.

Chapter 17: Finding Closure In Yourself

The quest for emotional healing often gets sabotaged seeking apologies, changed behavior, or restitution externally before feeling permission to make peace internally. But fulfilling such requirements of specific justice Ignores complex psychological dynamics keeping wounds fresh. True closure emerges from within by relinquishing victim status needing external validation. What personal practices foster self-directed healing?

The Apology Trap

Resentments naturally yearn for contrition through outward admittance of harms from offenders. We envision finally receiving accountability for wounds long denied which somehow promises to undo damage. Of course, factual honesty matters making amends interpersonally. But the fantasy that external confessions directly heal traumatic injury rarely matches reality.

Public proceedings demonstrate how even the most vile institutions – genocidal governments, abusive religions, law enforcement miscarriages – acknowledge horrific violations formally, yet still fail satiating victims and families wronged. Rarely does the long awaited testimony itself erase survival pain now woven into identity. Truer restoration requires looking inward where the seeds of suffering originally took hold.

Self forgiveness remains the only space where you alone can mend psychological wounds through compassion. Perpetrators may admit faults eventually, systems reform egregiously late or legal justice arrive posthumously. But peace stands independent of timelines through mastering inner ...reconciliation first. Consider what that path offers

Reclaiming Your Power

As tempting as it feels blaming villains who caused harm, recognizing shared humanity even in those committing ignorance frees inner turmoil far better long-term. Hurts happen; nothing personalizes victimhood permanently unless we permit it unconsciously. All struggle sharing similar core .needs beyond surface behaviors

Likewise, by taking self accountable for any subtle enabling tendencies – poor boundaries, naïve trust, passive communication – new wisdom protects you moving forward without embittering anyone. The goal dwells not in scolding abuse tactics but fostering understanding for mutual growth .and healing

Research confirms generating empathy even for perpetrators and focusing proactively on one's past role cultivated courage and resilience in Holocaust survivors. The material outcomes cannot change. But rewriting personal narratives around experiences surely can. Consider what power you actually ...possess

Owning Your Origin Story

Unprocessed memories maintain Intensity because the child ego, frozen developmentally when trauma occurred, perpetually projects nightmarish details trying to resolve frightening inconsistencies. The helpless two year old still weeps somewhere within adult consciousness.

But summoning that Innocent wise self today and comfortIng frustrations, providing stability missed back then reconciles the split. Say "You did nothing wrong. You deserved affection and still do." Make it conscious. Verbally declare no ghost from yesterday now holds power over your present choices proceeding peacefully.

Then purposefully re-author disempowering old Identity stories that linger. "I am stupid for ignoring red flags" gets purposefully transformed into "I courageously overcame adversity, wiser for it". "I should regret my mistakes" converts to "I gained principles navigating challenging dilemmas."

As Mandela attested "I am the master of my fate, I am the captain of my soul." Outcome fairness cannot get guaranteed. But proactively upgrading internalized narratives preserves sanity despite unjust odds.EXTERNAL EVENTS NEVER FULLY CONTROL personal freedom 100%. The Interpretations alone chain or liberate long-term. Mental flexibility endures beyond all.

The Dilemma of Forgiveness

For major emotional injuries, forgiveness seems an impossibly high standard to expect of victims. Yet holding onto resentment or awaiting restitution just perpetuates pain too. This dilemma leaves many feeling trapped in limbo unable to fully move forward yet exhausted by anger's toxicity. What alternative paths bring resolution?

Consider forgiveness as a unilateral personal act first rather than bilateral reconciliation needing recipient consent. Release hatred while still maintaining distance or boundaries from unhealthy associations. Forgiveness means absorbing the damage done without passing it on further - quite different than excusing harm inflictors from accountability. We call this "reflexive forgiveness" - an internal act of self care rather than pardon requiring dialogue.

Additionally, global spiritual traditions teach foreswearing resentment not for the sake of absolving offenders irresponsibly, but rather yourself from hostage bondage. As Buddha described "Holding onto anger is like grasping a hot coal planning to throw it at somebody else - you end up burning only yourself." Bombard those who harmed you with blessings Instead and feel palpable relief.

For giving extremely traumatic violations though, even reflexive forgiveness may understandably require extensive inner work over years before feeling achievable. Alternatively consider momentarily releasing pain during mindfulness rather than perpetual pardoning. Visualize destructive emotional energy dissolving as temporary relief. Healing happens .gradually

Cultivating Self-Trust and Intuition

Since breaches of trust usually accompany major wounds, dispelling lingering hypervigilance ultimately requires taking a second 'developmental leap of faith' in yourself as guardian of wellbeing going forward. The Instinct screams foolhardy before sufficient self-knowledge builds. But genuine agency .awaits on the other side

Experiment relying on your inner wisdom to orient confidently during adversity, not others' validation. What interests organically seem fulfilling whether or not surrounding folks approve? What relationships reflect your maturing needs regardless external narratives? What principles guide decisions ?aligned with your ethics now not caretakers from childhood

Lean fully into this unfolding new paradigm tribe without requiring consensus. Gradually self-reliance gets reinforced neurologically through simply showing up intentionally as your own caretaker over and over through uncertainty. Like parenting your inner child, absorb the blows of the world while refusing to lash out defensively. Newfound agency brings .closure at last

Here are three case studies showcasing finding Inner peace without external apologies or forgiveness:

Releasing Anger After Infidelity

Kia discovered her husband's affair after 10 years of marriage. Though outraged initially, obsessing for his apology stalled her healing. She realized blaming him ignored why she tolerated subtle disrespect quietly before. Through counseling, Kia built self-worth no longer abandoning needs for company. She nurtured independence rediscovering passions aside from the role of wife. Releasing anger, Kia felt confident divorcing respectfully without attacking character. She found peace loving her ex compassionately from afar while forging ahead on her journey. Kia learned not to weaponize past hurts, but grow through them.

Closure After Parental Neglect

Jamal's absent dad and alcoholic mom left emotional voids. He craved their apologies to fill inner emptiness. But when no contrition arrived, Jamal stayed angry for decades. In therapy, he practiced self-forgiveness for childhood coping mechanisms that became unhealthy in adulthood. By grieving the inner child's unmet needs, Jamal could parent himself today with compassion. Gradually he found closure by focusing energy into community mentorships rather than chasing validation from uninvolved parents. Jamal learned he could create the caring connections he always wanted.

MAKING PEACE AFTER Betrayal

Grace uncovered her business partner had secretly stolen company funds. Furious about the betrayal, she fixated daily on revenge fantasies. However plotting retaliation didn't reduce her sense of violation. Instead Grace found freedom by setting firm boundaries, exiting the business relationship without drama, then channeling anger into boldly starting over wiser. Investing in new trustworthy partnerships eased loss and made the future bright again. Grace learned she had power to move on rather than dwell in victimhood needing penance.

The Role of Self-Acceptance

Recovering from any profound loss or life upsets rarely follows linear neat stages culminating in acceptance. Grief and pain deliver unpredictable waves of anger, sadness, disorientation. Yet we unjustly characterize perfectly normal reactions as pathological "stuckness". This self-inflicted judgment then obstructs mourning by shaming its messy process.

Radically accepting imperfect healing progression and so called "negative" emotions allows spaces for nuanced shifts missed when demanding standard closure. Be patient and forgiving with setbacks or lingering hurt years later even. Consider emotion still surfacing a sign of openness and courage to feel at all when numbness often disguises unreconciled loss initially.

Honor feelings still demanding processing years later rather than ignoring their call. Verbalize your experience without judgment or needing it fixed. "I still feel abandoned when remembering my parent's negligence." Even lingering pangs of grief or bitterness get validated versus internalizing blame that you can't "move on from the past." Emotions themselves always lead somewhere meaningful. Trust in their sacredness.

The Power of Ceremony

Indigenous rituals demonstrate elaborate ceremonies focused on collective mourning unapologetically. Through gatherings specifically welcoming painful feeling states soulfully, public intimacy helps integrate loss into new identity stories transformed by the fires of suffering itself.

While Western cultural norms encourage stoicism and closure, coming together communally in feeling honors what remains unreconciled still needing witness. Creative avenues also hold space like music, poetry, gardening as living altars symbolizing both death and rebirth simultaneously.

Consider crafting resonant rituals for your process – composting keepsakes from the past, building memorial spaces in nature or dedicating creative works to what you are releasing. Infuse care and creativity into acts of letting go without rushed expectations. You lived whole lifetimes in those chapters now closing. The fullness of that journey deserves honor.

Reframing Timelines of Loss

After devastating life changes, consciously reclaiming stability and control often motivates hurry to just "get over it" by certain rigid deadlines. This false illusion suggests chapters of pain should neatly bookend allowing seamless continuation of "real life". Yet embracing emotional wilderness reminds that loss fundamentally transforms what awaits on the other side. Integration takes timelessness.

Consider this perspective: Forever imprinted by the immense gravity of pivotal turning points, identity itself evolves through mourning. One emerges as essentially a new being, revolutionized by the very rupturing of old worlds that came before. The timeline cares not for human impatience. Sacred alchemy works slowly but deliberately to reconstitute meaning itself from life's ashes. Stay tender with your timing.

When External Apologies Don't Arrive

Despite best efforts establishing boundaries, seeking accountability or even extending generous space waiting for people's awareness to grow around harms enacted, amend making communication remains elusive for some. Especially regarding vulnerabilities like abuse or neglect inflicted by close ties never acknowledging damage done, it provokes deep powerlessness.

Yet glimmers of closure emerge by ceasing over expending precious life energy chasing illusions of justice, restitution or even owes apologies from those unwilling. Instead invest solely into those reciprocating care now. Where can you sensitively attend your past and current suffering? What brings small measures of peace independently? Healing happens through changing the inner conversation. Modify self talk asking "What do I need?" rather than endlessly "Why won't they change?" Honor emotional echoes so they can integrate in readiness for you to step into long awaited freedom.

Chapter 18: Responding vs. Reacting to Challenges

A life without boundary violations, conflicts, hurt feelings, or disappointments sounds ideal. But facing interpersonal messiness often signifies the dawn of awakening if we harness reactions constructively. Rather than reflexively reacting to inevitable challenges from ego's defenses, pausing first cultivates empowered responding instead. What practices make space for poised grace under fire?

Recognize emotions without identifying

In triggering situations our logical brains get hijacked by primitive neural wiring priming reactive attack, numb withdrawal or collapse. Familiar emotions like anger, anxiety, resentment or sadness flood awareness instantly. But rather than fusing identity tightly with feelings, create space by gently noticing "I feel angry now" rather than declaring "I am angry!" Perceive the emotion's transient presence without personalization. Saying hello diffuses intensity faster than pretending not there.

Get radically curious

Once explosive emotions no longer possess consciousness absolutely, ask open ended questions non-judgmentally. Why specifically did my stomach sink hearing that? How exactly am I interpreting their words to spark defensiveness? Empathically investigate roots beneath immediate experience without accusation. Radical curiosity transforms villains into unaware teachers unlocking self-knowledge about sensitivities requiring care. Their delivery may have been poor, but fears exposed now ask for soothing. Mine for gold in disruptive moments.

Practice principled pausing

In stressful exchanges most tragically act on impulse defending righteousness without pause. Skilled communicators deliberately slow down by forcing not just long exhales but timed delays before replying. Pause for two minutes, two hours or even two days contemplating best steps aligning values before reacting. Create buffers preventing wounds inflicted onto you getting passed on thoughtlessly. Such principled self discipline builds trust eventually expected even under duress. We embody desired change first.

Master graceful boundary setting

Repeated misunderstandings signal the need for reinforcing respectful relationships by clearly reiterating healthy limits unapologetically. State boundaries without defining the offenders' intentions. "I cannot tolerate yelling. Let's take space and try discussing later." Then immediately enact stated consequences not permitting manipulation like "You always overreact" to distort your reality. Managing violations earlier prevents buildup exploding later disproportionately. Disagree with dignity.

Rewrite disempowered stories

Our perception of reality proves ever shaped by the narratives we construct about self, others and life. Getting passively victimized in an "unjust world" feeds helplessness inviting misuse repeatedly. But intentionally rewriting personal stories emphasizes agency. "Challenges help me clarify priorities and know myself more deeply" liberates. Befriend adversity as teacher through lens of growth, not punishment by villains deliberately targeting you. Heroes courageously transform trials into power.

Turn wounds into wisdom

Viktor Frankl, renowned psychiatrist enduring Nazi death camps famously attested, "Everything can be taken from a man but one thing: the last of the human freedoms – to choose one's attitude in any given set of circumstances." Hardiness research confirms trauma gets transcended when global meaning gets assigned to suffering. Consider volunteering for causes aiding populations who faced similar troubles. Helping other victims integrate pain builds hope and purpose from your wounds. We survive anything transforming agonies into mission. Thriving awaits beyond mere recovering by intentionally responding to life's complex challenges with skill and soul.

The Power of Rituals

Importantly, masterfully responding in the turbulent moments of conflict represents only part of sustainable transformation. Equally critical involves purposefully resetting the nervous system once flooding subsides. Deliberate self-care rituals signal safety from perceived threats restoring equilibrium literally neurobiologically.

Those best communing with unavoidable change in nature demonstrate the art of rituals: undulating palms bending without resistance to hurricane winds where rigid trees tragically topple under pressure. Adaptive resilience necessitates fluid wholesomeness.

Consider immediately after verbal arguments specifically interrupting biological stress activation that lingers through activities producing opposite physiology. Literally counterbalance tension by:

- Taking calming foot soaks while breathing slowly

- Massaging hands/feet with essential oils

- Sipping herbal teas listening to peaceful music

- Taking restorative yoga poses gently stretching muscles

- Walking shoeless on grass/sand tuning senses to beauty

Equally explore ritualizing the sacred inner terrain fractured by violations of trust through emotive writing, painting shadow aspects for integration or singing mournfully for closure. Creatively purge turmoil intentionally until felt senses get nurtured back to wholeness.

Honor wounds incurred rather than downplaying as inconsequential through dismissiveness. But also acknowledge that identity stands so much larger than momentary roles of victim when trauma strikes. You always retain sovereign choice pausing before reaction, responding skillfully then restoring whole beingness through self-care practices that explicitly bless inherent magnificence nothing can ever steal. Claim this grace as birthright.

The Freedom of Non-Attachment

Recurring problems also signal attachments unconsciously feeding repetition compulsions. Addictively craving approval, getting the last word or defending righteousness maintains entanglements even with those long walks away would liberate. Consider which ego hooks snag you.

Buddhist philosophy rightfully emphasizes clinging attachment itself as the root of misery when inevitably impermanent things change or people withdraw expected validation. Holding life conditions or relationships loosely allows going with natural flow rather than resistance exhausting vitality over what cannot get controlled. How much effort gets wasted trying to manipulate endings not authored by you? Where could that energy get better invested in creating beauty purely for its inherent sake absent needing anything in return?

Beyond circumstantial attachments, investigating the privileges and self importance lent narrative stories reveals a major key for responding over reacting. Catch self-concepts claiming "I'm above dealing with conflict poorly" or similarly positioning your dignity as unquestionably noble. The intensity of defensiveness relates directly to the inflated specialness assumed as identity. Healthy self esteem rests not in attainments but inherency. Then no criticism or perceived injustice lands existentially threatening defaults reacting angrily. Remain open handed receiving all feedback about ways to improve instead through humility and wisdom.

Cultivating Growth Mindset in Conflicts

Viewing clashes and disagreements through a lens of curiosity rather than judgment keeps perspective flexible for creative solutions. By asking exploratory questions, we shift from reactive postures to empowered responsibility for co-creating better dynamics. Consider the following prompts:

- Why might someone behave this way unconsciously? What inner hurts or unmet needs prompt them?

- How can I interpret this more positively rather than personalizing negativity?

- What could I learn about healthy relating from hearing out their experience?

- What vulnerability or sensitivity got exposed in me from this situation that requests more care?

- How might this disagreement contain wrapped blessings not yet visible to me?

- What boundaries or tone seem appropriate to model moving forward inviting their respect?

The motifs dwell not in faultfinding but seeking understanding. Examine the inner world rather than just outward behaviors. Help people feel felt through empathy. Discover universal human truths binding you in shared frailty and courage despite surface conflicts.

Even intense violations of trust like cruelty, deception or betrayal hide potential gold if interrogated as teachers rather than enemies. Consider themes exposed for you to mature – overly naïve trust, poor screening, ignoring red flags, people pleasing conflict avoidance. Then fortify those areas within rather than resenting the gift of illuminated weaknesses.

Of course certain toxic patterns defy salvage needing departure once attempts at mutual growth exhaust. Yet even then, adopt beginner's mind releasing bitterness quickly. Remain perpetually humble learning through clashes of personality, priority or viewpoint how to keep showing up wiser with each new souls encountered. What gem awaits being revealed to you next time? The journey continues...

Turning Mindfulness Into Habit

Implementing purposeful responding beyond just conceptual comprehension requires lifestyle integration through ongoing habits retraining reactive neural circuitry. What specific practices foster embodiment shifting not just ideas about reactive patterns but actual emotional reflexes to triggers?

Journal About Challenges

Journaling about real conflicts experienced proves one of the most effective methods for digesting upsets through a growth oriented lens safe from raw emotions present in the heat. Dedicate 10-15 minutes to reflect on a recent disagreement or boundary violation 1-3 days later once intensity settles. Explore:

- What core feelings got stirred up and what past situations evoke similar wounds now needing attention?

- How might I generously interpret their behavior through a compassionate lens? What suffering or unmet needs prompt them?

- What could I learn or change approach wise for increased harmony? How were my reactions driven by ego shadows versus values?

- How can I reframe disempowered narratives into opportunities clarifying self-care priorities going ahead wiser?

VERBAL PROCESSING WITH Friends

Beyond private written examination, verbally recounting challenging interactions to close allies Leads to profound clarity through a blended lens integrating their valuable outside objectivity alongside your own lived, felt experience. Often friends spotlight overlooked distortions or care suggestions in an empowering approach.

Schedule conversational space to review conflicts calmly after some time has passed. Explore their perceptions around all sides disturbed, assumptions made, who feels responsible to restore harmony first or opportunities for actual mutual growth somehow. Thank them for holding space to see your expanding edges while also championing your ongoing courage during difficulties life will surely keep delivering. Feel replenished by caring community holding complexity compassionately together.

SOMATIC RETRAINING Exercises

Cognitively reframing reactions proves only half the task with intense triggers. Equally urgent involves somatic reconditioning to prevent emotions like anger, anxiety or defensiveness from getting triggered so quickly physiologically even if conscious understanding expands mentally.

Here somatic psychology offers tangible practices:

- Place one hand gently over abdomen, slowing breath down while recalling disputes that still feel messy. Pause whenever anger surges. Place both feet into contact with the ground to feel gravity's support.

- During conversations that grow emotionally heated, pause to physically touch nearby objects signaling present moment awareness checking out from escalating intensity. Feel their textures reassuring embodied safety no threat now exists literally.

***

THESE PHYSIOLOGICAL rituals train nervous system regulation when typically reasoning shuts down flooded by adrenaline, cortisol or painful emotions from the past fueling reactions today. Appeal to the body directly. Let safety slowly soak into being until mastering presence regardless what gets spoken in worries, accusations or bounded fear appearing externally as "threats" thundering within.

Role Playing Difficult Exchanges

Finally, directly rehearsing challenging conversations in advance to experiment with alternative responses often reveals liberating new paths increasing mutual understanding. We never develop skill without practice – whether music, sport or relational disputes.

Ask a trusted friend to role play being the person you typically react emotionally towards. Or embody that critical voice yourself. Then mindfully attempt expressing boundaries, care for impacts, curiosity about their side or common humanity appealing to conscience from compassion not bitterness. Pause the exchange to discuss what worked, what requires polish and replay until body and spirit aligns with wisdom.

Through devoted practice you will gradually replace reactive habits with responsive empowerment. New neural pathways open as old relational fears heal. And you'll emerge ready to gracefully handle life's inevitable messiness through hard won skill specially trained for co-creating harmony.

Chapter 19: Focusing on Gratitude, Joy and Personal Growth

<hr>

Mastering inner peace through radical forgiveness, staying mindfully present and conscious responding liberates us to direct energy into positive domains like greater gratefulness, purpose and continual growth. What mindset shifts and practices directly nurture these fruits flowering everyday?

Gratitude's Transformative Power

Both spiritual traditions and scientific research reveal gratitude profoundly multiplies both external rewards and inner wellbeing long term. Beyond just formalizing thanks regularly, truly integrating deep appreciation habitually seeds optimal health, performance, relationships and even financial blessings.

A massive Harvard Study examining "what constitutes a good life" for 75 years concluded that cultivating gratitude trumped IQ, social class origins, genetics or professional success as the biggest determinant for thriving and fulfilment through all seasons of life.

The mechanics get revealed examining neural changes gratitude stimulation activates. Thanking others for kind acts or accomplishments makes us feel cared for reducing our sense of threat and isolation – a key predictor of disease according to researchers. Journaling gratitude also shifts perspective away from comparing/lacking into abundant contentment reducing urges toward addition, debt and status treadmills trying to cope with unmet inner needs.

We all enjoy receiving surprises, vacations or gifts. But transforming relationships plus life outlook substantially happens by focusing on blessing others daily through simple generous acts, keenly noticing their strengths and expressing genuine appreciation consistently. Tune in now...

Three Paths for Daily Gratitude Practice:

1. Thank before sleeping by listing 3-5 moments that day you feel grateful for: a smile from a stranger, tasty meal or getting an assignment completed. Such consistent practice physically rewires neural pathways prioritizing positives over threats keeping heart at peace as you rest.

1. Praise virtues and express care for loved ones freely. Delightedly share "I appreciate how dedicated you are Jeremy always supporting your team" or "You exude such wisdom and warmth Carol – thanks for being my friend!" Uplift people continually and notice bonds strengthen through thick and thin.

1. Each evening reflect specifically how difficulties or unwanted events still contained hidden blessings – resiliency became strengthened meeting workplace

challenges head on or unexpected free time let you enjoy hobby creativity revitalizing inspiration. Actively seeking the blessings in each circumstance deepens faith in life's care for you.

TRY ONE GRATITUDE HABIT (or all three) for the next 30 days observing life's transformation unfold subtly both internally and externally as continues beyond. When made habitual, thankfulness completely changes the game. Now let's explore how embracing larger goals and growth mindsets weaves all of life's threads into meaning...

The Fulfillment of Continual Growth

Psychologists find that nothing combats emptiness and anxiety over external conditions we cannot control like committing to intentional growth around inner strengths and life purpose. Those focused continually on self improvement, contributing talents to help others and expanding wisdom through mistakes consistently report the highest levels of life satisfaction and resilience.

The Japanese call this Golden Circle model Ikigai: finding flow in the sweet spot intersecting what you're good at, what you can get paid doing, what the world needs and what personally fulfills you long term. However discovering one's calling both through career and volunteering regularly requires patience trying new directions, befriending failures along the way graciously while monitoring internal signals pointing towards service. Growth depends not on arriving but through courage to progress imperfectly beyond past limitations time and again.

Fulfillment rewards those improving 1% daily – trying new recipes, reading books on interesting topics nightly before bed, showing up more patiently despite recurring mess ups again, brainstorming entrepreneurial solutions for environmental problems needing better options. All progress however small compounds, building identity not requiring outward praise. Keep expanding edges without judgement, learn from elders ahead and mentors behind. The purposeful life waits assembled fully present.

FROM BULLIED TEEN TO Anti-Bullying Coach

Sandra recalled with pain years getting mocked and shamed relentlessly about her appearance, second hand clothes and shy mannerisms. While academic scores stayed high in school soothing inner wounds somewhat, Sandra believed the projections whispered – she was stupid, ugly, unworthy of belonging.

After college Sandra first pursued work inbig law firms to prove worthiness through external success metrics. But 80 hour work weeks only compounded emptiness. Near breakdown, pivotal insight dawned that until self-acceptance healed from within, no outward attainments could satisfy the little girl still hurting.

Through intensive counseling then speaking engagements courageously sharing her story, Sandra organically discovered life purpose – empowering other bullied and outcast teens. Seeing their aha moments of self-worth touched her deeply full circle. She soon launched a nonprofit and book spreading the message she most needed younger. "Your beauty and brilliance deserve embracing exactly as you are right now. Together we'll uncover that bright light waiting for you too..."

From Startup Failure to Serial Entrepreneur

Raj was the classic struggling artist type in college bobbing around without direction trying on busker identities inconsistently – indie songwriter, travel blogger philosopher and temp jobs barely financing finding himself. His parents fretted when would their bright son get serious and exit years extended adolescence?

After the 2008 recession halted career mobility his friends enjoyed, Raj dusted off teenage dreams of entrepreneurship creating a startup merging music discovery and environmentalism. Six months hard work securing patents and angel investments turned devastating receiving news that bigger competitors won first rights to these models the very same week.

Losing his dear pet turtle earlier that year through neglect not budgeting proper healthcare already crushed Raj deeply. Now squandering years savings into a startup sinking so abruptly paralyzed all hope. The shame and despair nearly ended everything.

But after months hiding alone painting to process grief, Raj realized utter collapse contained his rebirth too – through compassionately understanding failures as teachers not tormentors. If his vision could not uplift the world exactly as planned, the worthy causes themselves remained and many paths still existed making contributions.

Raj began brainstorming ventures at the intersection of creativity, technology and ecology with friends which soon birthed a brilliant new startup employers loved. New patents got filed doubling income within 2 years. All because risking greatly unleashed innovation. Today Raj pays it forward mentoring other entrepreneurs through the valleys reminding panic often precedes victory.

From Burnout to Burnout Expert

Anita excelled being very driven – top of her Ivy League class, marketing magician earning rapid promotions and happily married navigating a bicoastal marriage no problem. She prided handling nonstop work travel, networking events until midnight plus passionately leading large teams experience without sacrificing workouts daily prioritizing self-care too. Her plate overflowed in success.

Until the year anatomy caught up through relentless migraines, adrenaline crashes, insomnia and finally a panic attack live onstage presenting ironically at a women's leadership conference. Utter public humiliation then desperately needing extended medical leave sparked long suppressed questions – when was the last time I stopped and enjoyed living rather than relentlessly producing? Was this nonstop drive my own or imposed since youth subtly?

Deeper healing came gradually through Anita courageously probing tough truths – impossible expectations seeking the world's approval to compensate for emotionally distant parents' validation withdrawn whenever Anita seemed anything less than perfect growing up. Radical self forgiveness for still trying to win invisible love freed energy towards building confidence internally instead.

Soon Anita found authentic joy rediscovering nonproductive pleasures like painting, dancing freely or laughing with friends between reasonable work hours. No longer depending solely on output for self worth allowed receiving loveliness in small glimpses of beauty surrounding her in the present.

And wonder of wonders, Anita's promotions accelerated again 2 years later as CEO of a Fortune 500! This time leadership got grounded in fierce compassion for all struggling to balance sane productivity, self care and staying true to inner wisdom. Her public story inspired millions.

The desire for self Improvement never ends. But realizing growth unfolds beyond worldly measures alone reclaims freedom to walk the ongoing path wholeheartedly present. What wondrous transformation awaits your next step too?

Learning Life's Lessons: Finding Growth in Loss

"A smooth sea never made a skilled sailor." Traversing difficult storms while maintaining integrity and vision expands our capacity thriving through all seasons. Seeing beyond surface setbacks to underlying invitations for gaining wisdom proves essential for progressing forward positively. How does heartache harvest happiness ultimately and how is deep peace restored after turmoil finally dissolves?

Honoring Grief's Wisdom

The crushing pain accompanying loss often immobilizes people indefinitely through shame, denial or self attack thinking we should hurriedly soldier on without properly integrating experiences first. But embracing emotional wilderness reminds that wounds fundamentally transform what awaits on the other side. Grieving prepares new ground so that joy may dwell richly again in time.

Rumi's classic words ring true: "The wound is the place where the Light enters you." Consider grief a teacher entering powerfully when death, accidents, violations or endings demand surrender and rebirth. Make space for this initiation through tears, raging, underwater silence and self examination without judgment. Interrogate pain for the growth lesson within. Inquiry holds hands with darker times so we surface renewed.

The Hero's Journey

Resilience gurus reference two prime narratives we unconsciously adopt dictating how reality gets framed: victim mentality bred from unjust affliction versus hero mentality strengthened through trials by fire. Befriending adversity as ally rather than enemy trying to diminish you creatively rechannels wounds into wisdom. Heroes allow challenges to expand empowerment.

Catch internal self talk after failures, conflicts or loss defaulting into disempowered stories: "I was attacked, betrayed and left damaged by life's cruelty" or similarly positioning yourself as merely recipient of external blows hammering self worth. Consciously re-author identity as brave protagonist on an epic quest: "This pain clarified my priorities ahead while illuminating strengths within to depend on regardless what gets taken." Claim courage and authorship.

The Phoenix Process

Post traumatic growth research reveals people often emerge renewed in unimagined ways with unexpected gifts and direction after immense hardships finally get integrated well. Like the mythical phoenix rising boldly from charred ashes where former lives perished, conscious participants in loss intentionally harness the alchemical fire burning away illusion so that wholeness Emerge's eventually. They apprentice suffering to uncover meaning.

What turned to ash in your world that actually made space for unforeseen blessings to come alive? The job loss or broken engagement redirecting towards truer vocations? The illness forcing self care resetting how you honor body and spirit? The national tragedy awakening political action or projects empowering communities vulnerable? Consider the phoenix's rebirth. Write fresh futures rising from the flames of your past.

A Second 'Leap of Faith'

As children the very first developmental leap into uncertainty rests with trusting caretakers — the basic safety net caught skillfully inspires toddlers towards independence. But when traumatic loss undermines such caregiver bonds through grief shattering protective shelters in our psyche, maturing requires taking an even more daring second 'leap of faith' now in oneself alone as guardian henceforth.

The path seems unfathomable initially. Yet genuine agency awaits on the other side by walking forward expectantly that direction gets illuminated step by step. Like parenting your inner child, absorb the blows of the world while refusing to lash out defensively. Model self assurance as the strong container. And never resist troubles when they visit but make wild peace with destiny's arriving unannounced. The new journey just begins...

Chapter 20: Transcending Tribalism

Beneath surface differences of ethnicity, nationality, religion or belief systems, all humanity shares universal bonds of love, suffering, hopes and dreams that unite us. Yet the mind habitually divides the world between tribal "us vs them" categories causing separation and conflict. How does transcending this illusion enable forgiveness, openness and social harmony?

The Roots of Prejudice

Social psychologists reveal much cruelty and oppression arises from cognitive distortions assigning insidious motives imagined in tribal "others" competing for resources and power. Leaders manipulate followers into blaming separate groups instead of corrupt systems causing inequality.

Even subtle prejudice colors how we perceive events like interpreting neutral expressions on different race faces as inherently more hostile. Brains unconsciously categorize unfamiliar people as threats simply due to novelty. Our nearest primate cousins attack or evade foreign creatures lacking distinguishable identity markers like themselves. Prejudice therefore gets called humanity's "original sin" persisting in collective shadows.

Of course truth lives in nuance – diversity brings both richness and misunderstanding. Some cultural boundaries and ethical discernment stay necessary guarding against harm. But frequent problems trace back to instinctive distrust towards generalized outsiders without recognizing shared essence. How to unwind this?

From Tolerance to Solidarity

Beyond just "tolerance" of surface level differences lies opportunity for mutuality – interdependence acknowledging unique cultures while jointly addressing universal needs. Solidarity builds through compassion – truly imagining lives in others shoes dissolving the illusion of disconnection. Curiosity leads to deeper relationship.

Research on effective prejudice reduction strategies confirms that promoting common identities proves far more effective than just critiquing biases. Spotlighting similarity touchstones like cherishing kids, longing for belonging, facing mortality builds resonance fast dissolving barriers. "They" become "us" quite swiftly after recognizing parallel trials of being human together beyond any labels hypnotizing separation delusions temporarily. Psychology echoes wisdom traditions here – only connection heals.

But default tendencies habitually forget this truth. When controversial events happen, knee jerk reactions condemn opponents as subhuman for behaving ignorantly. Yet outsider hostility only breeds defensiveness not change. What opens possibilities for reconciliation?

The Heart's Wisdom

Movements demonstrate that inviting opponents to share their authentic outlook opens doorways faster than arguing facts living emotionlessly in heads alone. Validating another's felt experience even while disagreeing with conclusions reengages relational goodwill over time much more effectively that critiquing misguided beliefs through raw debate.

Find common ground through universal emotions – all people value freedom, get outraged by perceived injustice, feel deprived when rights get violated or family threatened economically. Help clarified where intentions attempt upholding dignity albeit through questionable methods. The heart must be heard before minds transform. Dialogue digs for mutual understanding first.

Four Practices for Everyday Solidarity:

Catch conditioned categorizations and rehumanize people mentally.

Suspend judgment when exposed to polarized debates. Stay curious for truth on all sides.

Get to know an "outsider" through courageous warmth. Find similar hopes beyond differences.

Advocate for policies aiding groups unlike your identity, focusing on their suffering.

Even amidst difference, rediscover shared essence when relating to all people, groups and beings. Common humanity waits as living truth once illusion of disconnection dissipates fully. Keep sowing seeds of universal belonging and notice old tribalisms unraveling. The awakened world sings in harmonious chorus transcending ephemeral divides. Love alone remains lifting barriers one embrace at a time.

UNCOVERING HIDDEN BIASES

Introspective inner work proves essential for dismantling tribal thought patterns when left unchecked unconsciously. Bringing awareness to reflexive biases builds realization that distorted perceptions insidiously color Interactions with broader world requiring correction through vigilance and compassion .together

Audit Internal Assumptions

What hidden stereotypes might you carry about disadvantaged groups that leak Into behaviors unintentionally? Sociologists encourage writing down instant associations when naming identities different than yours, then interrogating why certain .qualities come up unquestioned

Do visualizations of marginalized communities invoke traits like dirty, dangerous or morally deficient without credible objective proof? These projections often reveal internalized stigma from cultural narratives rather than factual truth about .diverse peoples. Be radically honest

Additionally assess places where discrimination shows up In subtler forms like telling homophobic jokes assuming no queer persons around to get offended. Or feeling anxious when unknown black teenagers wear hoodies occupy the same public spaces you frequent. Dissect microaggressions with bold .transparency even at personal discomfort for the sake of truth

.

The Impacts of Privilege

Responsible understanding also examines ignorance enabling unfair advantages certain dominant groups receive without consciously earning them. Class privilege for example affords financial ease rarely considering marginalized economic suffering day to day. Racial privilege breathes confidence of police encounters being respectful rather than life threatening .injustice endlessly feared

Critically analyze privilege beyond surface diversity credos. How are you actually complicit in unjust systems through complacency and assumption "others somehow deserve inequity" to justify comforts protective bubbles provide? Consider impacts daily actions could make creating more inclusive environments for disadvantaged and unseen groups. .Then tangible solidarity flows

Cultivating Cross Group Friendships

Psychologists confirm face to face friendships prove powerful dissolving prejudice towards groups demonized abstractly. The example of musician Daryl Davis personally befriending over

200 K members helps reveal Uncle Tom stereotypes as deeply caring individuals simply misguided by insulation and manipulated information. Grace and courage Invite transformation.

Seek opportunities building community across diverse circles: coaching sports for refugee kids, attending cultural holidays outside your experience, reading books profiling injustices still endured by minorities today amplifying compassion that turns passive ideals into responsive ally ship. Even small connections lead to rediscovering shared humanity in unlikely neighbors. Let walls between "us and them" melt through welcoming the strangers often feared.

The Soul and Role of Conflict

Crucially, conflict becomes inevitable and even healthy when engaging diversity sincerely beyond surface level acceptance. Suppressing tensions about complicated power dynamics provokes unconscious acting out often breeding more insidious prejudice eventually. Develop thick skin for clumsy communications, unskillful confrontations and immediate reconciliation misfires in order process tensions necessary exposing multidimensional truth. Stay at the table.

Model principled pluralism navigating disagreements with grace not escalation – calling in not out well meaning parties who cause unintentional harm. Assume growth intentions underlying all efforts however ignorant or offensive initially expressed. Create space for mutual forgiveness and willingness to change through sitting discomfort together. All great awakenings unfold through first reconciling estranged soul aspects to forge golden inner unity reflecting without. We are all each other's teachers in the end.

117

Chapter 21: Surrendering Control and Outcomes

Relinquishing attachment to needing specific results or tightly controlling external conditions proves profoundly countercultural yet supremely empowering. How does surrendering attachment to fantasied outcomes while taking inspired action unfold destiny more beautifully than limited ego plans alone?

Explore the paradoxical power unlocked when permitting life to surprise you. The relief and optimism coming from acceptance rather than fixation on preconceived ideals. Tools for avoiding projections about how situations "should be" to appreciate what actually unfolds.

Wisdom traditions contend all suffering springs from rejection of "what is" while pain recedes by affirming reality just as it is. The path of radical acceptance and trust. Ego plays small games seeking security while soul savors the eternal dance laughing, crying and resting in awe of every texture manifestation unfolds.

There are no wrong turns only new scenery. Everything converges to bless you when bitterness turns to trust. The art of flowing with rather than combating the intrinsic beauty of now. Presence as ultimate grail forever unlocking joy in the messy imperfect bloom of being alive.

Let go and let God" the adage suggests so easily - yet releasing"
the steering wheel of loved results and choreographed
conditions terrifies the ego fearing loss of control inside
unknown terrain. But by embracing reality as Innately
trustworthy despite appearances, life can unfold predictably
.more wondrously than we may plan solitary

Imagine what happened when you last set Idealized
expectations onto outcomes then clinged desperately needing
unremitting satisfaction guaranteed however events transpired.
Did frustration, disappointment or bitterness accumulate
when plans fell short? We suffer extremely endeavoring to
combat uncertainty life naturally provides through seasons of
.gain and loss, union and parting, achievement and failure alike

Instead, what relief follows loosening grips fixed needing joy to
arrive dependent on solely orchestrated circumstances? When
we stop trying to force life's wholeness Into bite-sized morsels
our hungry egos devour seeking lasting fulfillment in fleeting
pleasures alone. The compulsion for domination falls away
exhausted. We welcome unpredictable beauty that
.unremittingly surrounds

Yet the mind habitually forgets - fabricating detailed Images of
"the way to happiness" though joy itself forever remains elusive
in tomorrows once secured. We deny radiance directly present
behind obsession conjuring self-centered dreams awaiting

manifestation someday. Gradually we become possessed by our futile plans more than the glorious mystery gifting this and
.each moment afresh right now

Until pausing finally awakens us. We relinquish needing outcomes our way surrendering into the hands of timeless destiny operating, measure our grasping and taste freedom. Divine will exceeds mortal comprehension yet through
.oneness guides all perfectly

Release knowing smiles give way to flowing tears then laughter again. The clandestine nature of being. In secret stillness the fragments of life's tapestry weave together exquisitely even in challenge beyond fearful ways of narrow seeing. Endurance grows roots mysteriously and then gone one day soon without
.attachment

Herein the artless art of allowing unfolds - embracing sincere self-restraint and abandon simultaneously. Hold plans loosely as passing clouds destined for rain while wholly watering dreams hand in hand with providence. This elegant equipoise
.resides in each heartbeat awaiting activation once discovered

We come this way but once. How shall we Immerse fully into love's terrible beauty then passing elusive as a shooting star on summer eves? The secret power of surrender beckons subtly awakening...just let life breathe you unguarded into living
.prayer this moment enough

Chapter 22: Alchemy of Darkness – Transforming Inner Shadows

M ost fear the messy darkness within of unresolved traumas, embarrassing memories and undesirable qualities hiding from society's gaze. We suppress or deny unhealed aspects like rage, jealousy, hatred figuring banishing ugliness breeds wholeness insider. But wisdom traditions radically disagree – shadow integration instead releases freedom and power waiting activated from the inside out.

The Perils of Suppression

Just as our physical body manifests sickness forcibly ignoring issues needing care, our psyche equally suffers trying to purge troublesome emotions, limiting beliefs or unattractive impulses in vain hope of peace or perfection. This denial risks emotional fracturing from dissociating parts deemed "unacceptable." Like attempting to cut off your own hand, painful division backfires long term.

You see evidence already likely around secret vices pursued externally or explosively losing temper often. Consider brooding moods and depression also manifestations of anger turned inward after years silencing unmet needs appearing selfish or demanding vulnerability difficult expressing in childhood perhaps. Whether lingering sadness, cheating habits or blinded overreactions, shadows enact unhealthy outlets desperately begging illumination. The wounds require proper cleaning for hopes of healing ahead. This becomes our soul task...

OWNING YOUR GOLDEN Shadow

Cutting edge coaches and therapists urge courageously befriending your darkness first before positive transformation unfolds. The ignored, denied or hidden dimensions demand gentle attention like orphaned children seeking caretakers translating their veiled dreams into conscious speech. What wants understanding or creative redirection?

I invite you to get curious about your golden shadow now. Welcome home all emotions, behaviors and beliefs hiding from the light but awaiting acceptance. This denial enacts immeasurable suffering and isolation. But embracing the full truth of who you have been, are today and might yet become sets you free into radically whole presence. Wholeness heals everything.

The Masks We Wear

Transitioning from ego identity into true self first involves recognizing surplus armor built to secure love by hiding flaws. Consider the earliest coping mechanisms manifesting unconscious masks worn habitually ever since harsh lessons imprinted that honest emotional needs get attacked if openly expressed. So innocence masked adaptively...

Perfectionistic overachiever modes deny vulnerability covering up belief of inadequacy deep down. Or self silencing people pleasers bury anger unjustly attacking healthy boundaries before. Learn too the manipulator, victim, clown masks viele other inner fractures splitting authenticity into socially acceptable fragments instead of integrated flowing. There exists only light and love ahead. Be gentle but bold removing filters dimming your shine now.

Befriending Your Demons

Next assemble perceived flaws, embarrassing memories and other disowned aspects for conversation making space to meet life's messiness without judgment. Perhaps envy towards friends with easier childhoods sits buried under spiritual platitudes. Or old addictions still haunt subtly despite contrary identity externalized long ago. There exists no hierarchy for emotions. All ask kind witnessing.

Catalog every side thought judged wrong, secret impulse, brokenness felt sinful. Welcome split dark feminine Lilith alongside innocent Eve alike. Make fear, hatred, lust your allies through understanding why they served you once and how to alchemize energies more constructively henceforth. Shadows transfigure rapidly receiving caring hospitality meeting darkness directly with bravery and compassion. You discover that heaven hides waiting behind hell dancing ahead.

Integrate Psychic Fragmentation

Additionally when traumatic events overwhelm vulnerable nervous systems, psychologists recognize survival impulse fractures psyche into isolated emotional parts unable to process overwhelming stimuli completely. The abandoned child self segment parks unconsciously replaying scenes trying to resolve scary inconsistencies until caretakers internally integrate experiences through presence.

Implied here means gently dialogue with your inner child still frozen in time needing reassurance today. Soothe old wounds now conscious. Promise to protect, provide stability and celebrate playful innocence again safe. By carrying past burden compassionately, lightness lifts the adult journey onwards. All time unifies into singularity the moment we claim this power. The present heals all.

The Alchemy of Owning Shadows

Emerging research into post traumatic growth mechanisms confirms openly engaging personal shadows like moral failures, destructive behaviors or suppressed psychic content profoundly renews identity by dissolving denial. The darkness holds tremendous light once digested properly through courage and care. Discovering golden qualities prove inseparable from transmuting fear and weakness inside out. Wholeness waits here as our natural state of being.

But crux moves hinge misidentifying stories of unworthiness, inadequacy or irredeemably condemned. We witness messy humanity without fusing one's being with appearances and behaviors. Attach no labels permanently since essence ever remains untouched, whole and pristinely pure behind churning phenomena awakening unconditional love as natural awareness. Everything becomes blessing unmasked at last. The deepest truths set you free now.

The Pitfalls of Positivity Culture

In recent decades, mass fixation on manifesting lives filled purely with happiness, success and nonstop abundance grew popular in self help narratives. But critics argue blindly chasing positivist fantasies breeds isolation and self condemnation when reality includes loss, failures and emotional messes too. Discernment matters balancing mature optimism with radically accepting all spectrum of experience as teachers.

Consider the coach relentlessly challenging clients to "think positively!" when grieving loss or misfortune. The denial stems from fear that acknowledging wounded aspects risks being defined as damaged, rather than inherent wholeness waiting embraced. Further the law of attraction movement implies we somehow attract misfortunes through unconscious negativity or doubts manifested tangibly – a dangerous blame tactic entities like cancer patients face already unfairly by societies seeking tidy cause and effect.

Beyond positivity culture's toxic byproducts, hiding shadows proves delusional and dissociative. Traumatic events recur symbolically begging healing consciously through healthy processing. And rejecting grief, disappointment, uncertainty or other labeled unpleasant emotions ironically amplifies suffering by resisting innate flow states wanting expression before integration into whole beingness.

Can positivity exist sustaining grounded in reality's actual textures noted calmly or does it manifest naively floating cut off from the messy, chaotic tenderness belonging with humanness fully felt? Consider a new path valuing tears as the companion of joy alike...

The Signals Behind Anxiety and Depression

Just as physical injury announces something requiring care through pain, ongoing research spotlights how depression and anxiety function equally as messengers of unmet needs wanting attention whether emotional support lacking or wearing social facades misaligned from authentic spirit. Survival instincts embed reactions when core aspects feel threatened psychologically too.

But culture wrongly convinces us to pop pills deafening messages emotions carry rather than skillfully interpreting root causes for integration. Medicines do temporarily reduce difficult symptoms granting space to heal. Yet nested issues decree listening reflectively before any lasting peace found.

We must make the unconscious conscious through practices examining feedback loops from somatic cues and resistant behaviors manifesting daily. Radically probe what escalates your mood shifts – is grief still crying for witnessing? Does self silencing suppress bold expression? Might people pleasing tendencies deny personal needs or boundaries violated that require voicing now for liberation ahead? Lean into expansive healing.

The Courage Path of Vulnerability

Ironically the very act of denying supposed flaws and aspects deemed shameful actually generates exponential suffering rather than the intended separation sometimes necessary from destructive traits. Hiding instead robs us of our inherent beauty waiting actualized by fully owning the purposeful Middle Path walking between reckless shadow acting out and disconnected spiritual bypassing.

What awaits embracing messy, complicated and utterly imperfect human experience with compassion? The vulnerability and divine courage claiming one's whole truth warts exposed and wondered about? Beholding the primordial unity dancing here as consciousness loving all creations through temporary vessels and forms alike across the great unfolding.

Consider figural shapes gesturing from stone. The artist inside you witnesses latent grace awaiting chiseling rough facades until revealed at last. What wants to emerge from the cracks and scars of your journey too? This work remains the highest art freeing your most vulnerable power held captive awaiting bold liberation.

Review of Techniques

We covered extensive tools across this journey of mastering the art of letting go. As we prepare to depart, let's recap essential techniques revealed empowering you to:

- Release past hurts, grievances and regrets

- Manage unwelcome emotions with mindfulness

- Establish healthy personal boundaries

- Skillfully respond rather than react to life's difficulties

- Forgive yourself and others through understanding

- Discover blessings hidden within all circumstances

- Continually nurture personal and spiritual growth

Each chapter equipped practical wisdom grounded in ancient spiritual traditions and evidence based psychology research for transcending bitterness over betrayals; consciously working with "negative" emotions like fear, anger and anxiety; caring for sensitivities exposed during conflicts without attacking back; pivoting from victim mentality into creative responsibility through reframing stories empowering after hardships; appreciating the perfection of larger forces at play orchestrating experiences meant to mature our souls; and continually directing energy towards service and compassion.

We hope reviewing the roadmap overview here inspires you remembering the immense personal power available simply through releasing judgmental control and instead affirming life unfolding, feeling deeply, responding thoughtfully. Though outward rains may fall, discovering inner sunshine waits guaranteed the moment rigid expectations give way to fluid trust living awake here now.

Continuing the Journey of Letting Go

We never "arrive" fully with mastering life's intricate art of surrender and forgiveness. Unpredictable events relentlessly deliver new invitation practicing conscious mindfulness and understanding for all people and experiences showing up driving maturation. Yet now equipped with emotional tools and wisdom perspectives revealed in these pages, you stand ready to receive each unique opportunity growing empowerment and serenity increasingly through life's nonlinear journey.

Stay vigilant catching repetitive inner voices that hook destructive rumination cycles about painful histories. Use affirmations, body based practices and external accountability to short circuit unnecessary suffering mental time travel brings. You cannot change the past. But even genuine recognition of harm enacted offers sufficient balm rewriting inner narratives towards forgiveness. Bless and release love again without clauses.

Meet current adversities as whetstones keeping the blade of consciousness sharp – assessing emotional feedback signals mindfully without exaggeration, getting radically curious about growth lessons revealed for self and others alike by contrast teachers that enter unaware. We only mature rising to meet adversity with skills gained from past trials. Surrender shallow ego always seeking comfort. The peaceful heart knows only love remains.

Stay persistent yet patient with all beings and conditions as they mirror internal evolution. Consider every gift unique medicine assigned from beyond the veil specifically calibrated to reveal untapped potential yearning activation through provoked crisis. Lessons repeat until sufficiently grasped. There are no wrong turns now.

Trust life's underlying goodness and care while responsibly attending your energetic / emotional needs. The Universe endlessly gives again when we quit unconsciously tightening against uncertainty, lack or impermanence dwelling instead in faith and inspired action. Keep releasing, opening, forgiveness, leaning deep into this vast ocean of living presence surrounding all.

We are one eternal play of consciousness forever blessing itself emerging as individuals all. Go well awakened beings...your most joyful dance awaits beyond fear's trance fully understood at last. Always in all ways you remain held in unconditional light never separating true nature whole, healed and home here now. We surrender too...

The Journey Ahead

As we conclude this exploration into the art of letting go, remember that mastering Inner peace and forgiveness Is not a destination but an ongoing journey. Life will continue to challenge you with new difficulties, reversals, disagreements and losses. Yet now you stand equipped with practices and .perspectives for meeting any adversity with grace

The key Is maintaining faith that existence unfolds in our highest benefit even when temporarily unclear. Adapt nimbly without attachment to conditions being a certain way. Flow with unavoidable change accessing the space between thoughts where your eternal essence shines untouched by passing troubles. Keep planting seeds of empowerment, compassion for all beings, releasing judgment about yourself and others. Stay closely tuned to whispers of intuitive guidance supporting .next right action

You will stumble at times, forgetting wise ways thePulls of past conditioning get strong. When you find yourself grasping again wanting control things vainly, get curious about fears driving such fixation as the cue reminding realign with trust, .openness and inner peace Inherent

No matter what circumstances you face ahead, may you yet remain courageous enough to love immensely – yourself, neighbors both close and far and this wild unfolding mystery we call Life. The great dance ever births us anew the moment .we stop resisting the inherent perfection already here

Go well awakened one...your most joyful path awaits ahead the
.moment you choose. Always in all ways we remain together

THE END

About the Author

Hadi Hans is an aspiring young author who draws upon his rich life experiences in his writing ,Imarried with two lovely daughters named Lucine and Lorianne.

Hadi continues traveling extensively to fuel his literary passions, and draws daily inspiration from his diverse surroundings.

His rich global upbringing informs his empathy-driven stories.

desire to bridge divides between people via storytelling. His experiences grant authentic perspectives to his fiction.

The dream has always been to write books for children and adults as well.